40 Days to the Promise:
A Journey Through the Wilderness

by

Stan DeKoven, Ph.D.

ISBN: 1-931178-76-3
Copyright, Stan DeKoven, 1993

Vision Publishing
1520 Main Street, Suite C
Ramona, CA 92065
www.vision.edu

Second Edition, 2001
Third Edition, 2004

Scriptures taken from the
New American Standard Bible
and the New International Version
unless otherwise stated.

TABLE OF CONTENTS

ACKNOWLEDGMENT

I want to acknowledge so many people who have had an influence in the development and the transformation of my own character, something that is still very much in process.

First, thanks to my parents who brought much of my natural personality to the forefront through their parenting style.

Second, Dr. Bohac, my father in the faith who first introduced me to the concept of wandering in the wilderness and God's plan for bringing us to a place of wholeness and completeness.

My beloved Karen, now with the Lord!

My two precious daughters, Rebecca and Rachel. May you continue to walk in love and care as we continue life together in the promises of God that we have inherited through the Lord Jesus Christ.

Finally, for the many wounded saints who thought wilderness wandering was their life pursuit, there is hope. Your journey has purpose, and your destination in Christ assured. Trust Him!

AUTHOR'S FOREWORD

I was 19 years old when I first heard the analogy or typology of the children of Israel's exodus from Egypt and journey toward the Promised Land as a picture of our own spiritual journey.

Dr. Bohac taught a series of lessons that became so important to me in the formative years of my spiritual journey in the early 1970's.

If I remember it correctly, Dr. Bohac's perspective was that although God's plan was for all His people to enter the Promised Land there must come a time of traveling or traversing the wilderness in preparation for the inheritance of the Promises.

Most Christians know the picture or type presented in the Old Testament story of the Exodus. The children of Israel had been in bondage for 400 years. During that time the people prospered initially, but eventually they became slaves to the Egyptian Pharoah.

In the fullness of time, according to His Promises, God raised up a deliverer, Moses, who confronted the Pharaoh of Egypt, eventually won his reluctant permission for the release of the Israelites.

In this marvelous miracle of God's grace, mercy and power, you will learn several important lessons including:

1. Egypt is a type of sin and of bondage.
2. Moses was a type of deliverer, savior and mediator even as Christ.
3. Moses preached that there is liberty and freedom for those who are in bondage, as Christ preached.
4. The deliverance of the children of Israel through the Red Sea is a true type of trusting in the blood of Jesus.

The Israelites crossed the Red Sea and, after a brief time of rejoicing in the desert, began their trek toward Canaan, the land which God had promised to Abraham, Isaac, Jacob.

Between Egypt, which was the place of bondage, and the Promised Land, the place of inheritance, was the wilderness, a dry desert area filled with opportunities for blessing but also opportunities for failure.

Through Moses, the children of Israel received divine instructions, the Ten Commandments and the moral laws that they were to live by. God provided manna, water and everything else they needed to survive in the wilderness.

Dr. Bohac taught, and I agree, that it was not God's plan for the children of Israel to spend 40 years wandering in the wilderness. In fact, 40 days was more than enough time for the journey.

For all Christians there is of necessity a wilderness <u>experience</u> but <u>wandering</u> aimlessly through the wilderness is only for those who are disobedient or who lack wisdom, knowledge and understanding of God's perfect plan or purpose for their life.

This book reveals how you can successfully traverse the wilderness experience!

It is time the churches stopped denying the reality that all Christians must go through a wilderness experience. The experience is subsequent to their deliverance from sin.

In this book I will bring to the forefront the reality that you must go through this experience, and if you must go through it, God must have a plan to help you complete the process so that you are ready to inherit the Kingdom of God. Are you able to fully inherit the tremendous promises found in the Word?

We will look at specific plans to bring about changes in a person's life so that they might be conformed to the image of Christ. Our ultimate destination is Heaven. Between being born again and our final promotion is the Kingdom of God, which we have been born into. We have received righteousness, joy and peace by the Holy Spirit (Romans 14:17). We have been called of God to fulfill a destiny in Christ.

THE JOURNEY

It was relatively easy to get the children of Israel out of Egypt, the difficulty was to get to get Egypt out of them. Even after their miraculous deliverance they still carried a slave mentality. As slaves, many bad habits were learned; as free people new habits needed to be established. Because they did not walk obediently to the plan, and the purpose of God a whole generation perished in the wilderness.

As a Christian you have come out of Egypt (sin) but find it difficult to get Egypt (sin) out of your life. You need to put the old habits that ruled your life behind you. As a free person you must develop new habits. You need to establish an intimate walk with the Lord, to be grounded in the knowledge of God and become conformed to the image of Christ.

You need to become obedient to God's Word and dependent upon Him as the Source of your life. All of these things are necessary if you are to understand the process, the plan and the purpose of God for you.

Over the years many men and women who were miraculously delivered from sin and filled with the Holy Spirit have withered up in their wilderness experience and fallen by the wayside. It is my belief that, with God's help, you can conquer the wilderness experience with grace and strength.

In the wilderness you are forced to face the character issues of the heart. When you endure the pain of facing your own failures and overcome them you begin to inherit the promises of God.

For those who have accepted the assumption that there's a magic carpet ride from Egypt to Canaan, I hope you won't be too offended by the reality that for everyone there is a wilderness.

You must go through it. But... God's plan is for you to come through it as an individual whose mind and heart have been transformed and renewed in such a way that you can defeat your enemies and possess the land God has given you.

INTRODUCTION - HOW THIS BOOK BEGAN

It was a beautiful Monday morning as I drove toward my office in the center of San Diego, California.

Each day has its challenges, but none more challenging than that one!

Over the weekend a minister friend and fellow counselor suddenly died. Although the circumstances surrounding his death remained unclear, it was definitely a drug overdose that swept him into eternity.

My plan was to see a few clients then meet with a small group of friends to schedule a memorial service to his life and especially his ten years of ministry.

My friend had led hundreds to Christ and assisted scores of others in their recovery process from drug and alcohol addiction. We were gathering together as his friends to mourn this tragic loss.

As is my custom, I began to pray as I drove. However, my prayer became a cry of anguish to the Lord. I wanted to know why this warrior for Christ had given in to the devil's temptation. How could a minister of the Gospel who had led literally hundreds to Christ and discipled hundreds into the kingdom of God be suddenly cut off, even if by his own hand?

As I drove I reviewed in my mind the various theological suppositions, God's permissive will; man's free choice; and psychological theories, depression and despair leading to irrational acts or behavior; unresolved post-salvation conflict, etc.

None of the explanations brought solace to my troubled spirit. It was when I came to the end of my conjecture (isn't that most often when God speaks?) that I heard my Lord speak in clear revelation, "there's 40 days to my promise."

My mind attempted to comprehend but I didn't understand! I was however, smart enough to know that it was time to "be still" before the Lord and let Him speak. As I tearfully attempted to safely negotiate my driving tasks, I wrote down the outline for this book.

As tears streamed down my face God gave me some clues as to what He meant when He said, "there's 40 days to my promise." It took over 2 years from that visitation from the Lord before I was finally at liberty to release this book.

In simple terms the Lord put in my heart several seemingly disconnected concepts from theology, Bible history, psychology and personal experience. This book is a tool to assist Christians to conform to God's word and to prepare them for true Kingdom living.

No one is exempt from the wilderness, though many will try to avoid God's preparation either through ignorance or rebellion. This guide will help you understand and progress through the wilderness, it will lead you toward the Land of Promise.

Many ministers from around the world are telling us that God is raising up a Joshua generation. These leaders will be young men and women who will minister in God's power and possess the promises.

In light of this, it is important to remember that Joshua and Caleb endured the wilderness experience. They learned the necessary lessons, were hardened through harsh reality. They were equipped in the University in the wilderness to work the works of God and rout the enemies of the Lord.

It is my hope and belief that this material will minister deeply, especially to those who have been severely wounded by life's circumstances, to help propel them forward in their Christian experience to inherit the promises of God.

Further, it is my prayer that this book will be used by the Lord and

His Church to give breakthroughs, wholeness, healing and hope to the many wounded soldiers and leaders in the body of Christ.

A FURTHER THOUGHT

If you have asked Jesus to forgive you of your sins and cleanse you, the Holy Spirit lives within you. You are now a new creation in Christ, *"loved by God"*, *"accepted into His family"*, *"filled with His purpose"*, *"seated in the heavenlies with Christ"*, and the *"apple of His eye."*

"You are now a royal priesthood, a holy nation, and a peculiar (unique) *person."* When the Father proclaimed His favor on His Son, He was proclaiming the same upon all of His sons.

I am not talking about the portion of your salvation which parallels the entrance into heaven as our guarantee, but your continued growth in salvation to fulfill your place in His Kingdom. We are not yet what we shall be, but we are in process.

This book, properly used will help you in your greater preparation for God's kingdom service on earth.

HOW TO USE THIS BOOK

This book is best used by those who are first and foremost, hungry to grow in the things of God and to understand His process for change and growth. If you are searching for Truth and Light, you will find it very helpful.

It's important to read the first section of the book before beginning the process of applying what you will be taught through this study.

Once you have read about God's plan for the journey, what character transformation is all about and its importance in terms of our walk with Christ, you will be ready to apply what you have learned, through the "putting off and putting on" process.

A workbook section of the 20 primary issues of the heart that need to be laid aside, and the 20 primary characteristics of the new man that need to be put on, so that you can be all that God intended you to be, is provided for you. (Chapters 10 and 11).

I recommend that you not do the workbook alone unless that's the only way you can do it. It is always better to be in a relationship with a mature Christian who has been through a wilderness experience and can relate to you as an individual with confidentiality, love and care.

My hope is that you will find someone within your own local church to assist you. If you can't, search for a church where you can receive the help you need as you deal with the important issues of your heart.

This book can be a great blessing. It's not the answer to all human needs. No book is, except the Word of God. What is provided here is a systematic approach of facing the characteristics of your heart that must be dealt with and in doing so you are cooperating with the Holy Spirit who is the Revealer of all Truth. He will help you to be transformed and changed. That's the responsibility of the Holy Spirit.

If you become stuck in your process, if you find an area of life that disturbs you and causes you greater trouble than you can bear, it may be necessary to seek a higher level of professional help in the Christian community.

Should that be the case, don't become discouraged, all of us need assistance from time to time. You must be willing to reach out. Ask your pastor for additional help so that you can continue through the process. Remember, it is God's plan for you to live a victorious, complete, full life in Christ.

There are two sections to this manuscript which can be used in three different ways.

The first chapter, entitled "The Journey of 40's" outlines the Biblical basis of transformation, how character is formed and in some instances deformed, and the process of restoration and reconciliation found in the Word of God. Combined with that will be the procedure for your journey to the promises.

This book is designed to be used. It is most effective in a one, two or three discipleship relationship, preferably with someone who has gone through the "40 days to the Promise" journey. However, it can be quite effective in devotional style; just you and God, if you can be open and honest with the Lord and follow the book all the way through.

The companion book is a practical journal entitled, *Forty Days to the Promise Journal*, which I pray you will walk. Without the doing of the Word the hearing will be of no great effect (James 1:22-25).

The material can also be presented in a large group or seminar format but that is usually for instructional purposes. It is recommended that you utilize the companion workbook, *Forty Days to the Promise Journal* to receive the full impact of this teaching.

In either case, you must be willing to be vulnerable before the Lord and hopefully, one other mature, confident Christian will help you receive the maximum benefit.

The reason for this is accountability which is a vital part of your growth and maturity. Of course the Holy Spirit is perfectly capable of doing this through God's Word and circumstances.

My experience has been that all Christians, regardless of intelligence, psychological makeup, denomination, affiliation, race or culture, are going to experience a wilderness. Even our Lord Jesus Christ had to face it.

Your choice is crucial. Either you will take a wilderness experience precipitated by the leading of the Holy Spirit, assisted by a trained guide, and begin to inherit God's precious promises, or you will walk around in doubt and fear taking numerous trips around the mountain, only to waste 40 years in futility.

Time is short; the bridegroom is coming for His bride. The hour of your of preparation is now!

CHAPTER ONE

The Journey of 40's

Many people are fascinated with numbers. I've always been interested in people's ages. I try and match a person's appearance with their age, hoping that they are older than they look or at least older than me.

In the past I was never hung up on the whole concept of numerology, or numbers and their meaning in the Bible but once I had received this revelation from the Lord I wanted to know more about the significance of the number 40, if it had significance in relationship to change or to our journey in Christ.

I researched several sources finding the best material in Wilson's Dictionary of Bible Types by Walter Lewis Wilson (published by Eerdmans, 1957). He discusses in great detail the various references to the number 40 explaining that the number 40 seems to represent testing in human life, leading to transitions or change. That would certainly make sense in light of the children of Israel and the wilderness

They were the key players in a major change from being slaves with no real concept of being the true people of God, to inheriting the Promised Land. There are many references to the number 40 that seem to validate change.

A few of the important references are presented here to establish that this is not just a fly-by-night concept, but one based upon Biblical significance.

BIBLE REFERENCES

Prior to entering the ark of promise, a type of Christ's safety and salvation, Noah prepared for 120 years a multiple of three, forties. Once he was inside the ark the earth experienced 40 days and nights of rain which brought about a major change. The rest of humanity was completely destroyed and a brand new race began through the lineage of Noah.

The children of Israel were given a significant test of loyalty to God!

Rather than being grateful for God's provision, the heavenly manna, they desired leeks and garlic, the old food of Egypt. (Exodus 16:1-35; 24:18; 32:7) They also desired the safety of the desert in Kadesh-Barnea, a place of rest but not a place that God intended for His people to remain. God's plan was to take them, not on a 40 year desert wandering, but a 40 day walk, which is approximately what it would have taken to go from Egypt into the promised land had they taken the direct route.

Israel's failure of the test of loyalty meant an entire generation was lost. I honestly believe that if we fail to come to a place of obedience in Christ or fail to face the wilderness experience we will end up losing the purpose, plan and promises of God for our life.

There will be more on this in Chapter two, Ten Trials in the Wilderness.

We see MORE 40's in the life of Eli the High Priest

> *"And it came about when he mentioned the ark of God that Eli fell off the seat backward beside the gate, and his neck was broken and he died, for he was old and heavy. Thus he judged Israel forty years."* 1 Samuel 4:18

Because Eli was unable to deal with the problems of his own sons he experienced judgment on his sons and upon himself. Eli judged Israel for 40 years but he had failed miserably in the task of disciplining his children. He made no preparation for the next generation.

We see how Saul was tested in terms of his courage in dealing with Goliath:

"And the Philistine came forward morning and evening, for forty days, and took his stand." 1 Samuel 17:16

The Bible says that Goliath, the Philistine, came forward morning and evening for 40 days to take his stand against the children of Israel. During that time Saul wavered in terms of his willingness to confront the enemy of God. But a young man named David, a man full of faith and courage, under the anointing of the Holy Spirit, stood in place of King Saul and was able to slay Goliath.

This signified a change in the leadership, God's hand was taken from Saul and placed upon David and in the eyes of the people David became the leader of the nation of Israel. 2 Samuel 5:4 says that David reigned as the king (as a type of Christ) for 40 years. It was a victorious reign for him and Israel.

Despite David's sin with Bathsheba and his other failures, God blessed him and allowed him to be king over Judah and Israel for the 40 years.

After David's death, Solomon his son came to the throne and reigned in peace for 40 years:

"Thus the time that Solomon reigned in Jerusalem over all Israel was forty years." 1 Kings 11:42

Again there was a change from the 40 years of war and conquest under David to 40 years of peace and prosperity under Solomon.

It is important to note that the number 40 signifies probation, trial, even chastisement, not at the hands of enemies but to discipline us as sons and daughters.

Forty can also be from a combination of the numbers 5 and 8 which means revival or renewal, also to enlarge or to take dominion, to extend our rule. These are all things that God intends for us as His people.

Let's review and explore more areas in the Old Testament. You will find that there are 15 periods of 40 years of probation or trial. In

Deuteronomy 8:2-5 & Psalm 78 we see the wilderness experience of the children of Israel.

There were three 40 year periods of Moses' life; 40 years in Pharaoh's court, 40 years on the back side of the desert in preparation and 40 years of leadership as he brought the children of Israel through the wilderness to the entering of the Promised Land.

The Bible speaks of a 40 year rule of peace in the days of Othniel

(Judges 3:11). Then there was Deborah and Barak (Judges 5:31) and Gideon (Judges 8:28) each of these stories tell of 40 years of peace. The book of Judges also reveals 40 years of probation, prosperity, deliverance, and rest.

Strange as it may seem there were 40 years of problems during prosperity in the reign of King David, (2 Samuel 5:4) his son

Solomon, (1 Kings 11:42) and King Joash, (2 Kings 12:1-20; 13:3, 5, 7, 22; 14:12-14, 23, 28). There were 40 years of probation by humiliation and servitude under the rule of the Philistines, (Judges 13:1). King Saul was enthroned 40 years but those were not happy prosperous years (Acts 13:21).

There are many other places where the number 40 is discussed. For instance, Moses on the mountain receiving the law from God, (Exodus 24:18) also the 40 day period after the sin of the golden calf

(Deuteronomy 9:18, 25).

Israel wandered through the wilderness for 40 years (Numbers 13:26; 14:34). Elijah fasted for 40 days on Mt. Horeb (1 Kings 19:8). In the famous Biblical account of Jonah and the whale, Ninevah was given a 40 day window before destruction (Jonah 3:4). The Bible also says that Ezekiel laid on his right side 40 days to symbolize Judah's 40 years of transgressions (Ezekiel 4:5-6; 29:11).

Jesus was led of the Spirit into the wilderness where He fasted for

40 days and was tempted of the devil (Matthew 4:2). Between His resurrection and His ascension the Lord ministered and taught His disciples for forty days about the kingdom of God (Acts 1:2). From the crucifixion Christ to the destruction of Jerusalem was 40 years.

WILDERNESS EXPERIENCE

Jesus suffered the travail in preparation for His crucifixion. This time in the garden can be likened to His last great wilderness experience. John the beloved endured his time in the wilderness on the Isle of Patmos and Paul the Apostle was thrown into prison.

The fact is all humanity goes through a time in the wilderness. As I mentioned earlier, we either go through it with grace, believing in and relying on the mercy of God or we go through it kicking and screaming. It is easy to miss the promises of God and make the wilderness a life journey like the children of Israel did.

Jamie Buckingham wrote a book in 1983 called *A Way Through the Wilderness*. It's an excellent book in which he provides keen insights from his many journeys in the actual wilderness where the children of Israel wandered.

There are several quotes that I'd like to present which I think are excellent for your study in *40 Days to the Promise*.

Quote: "The tragedy of our wilderness experience is not that we have to go through grief and suffering but that we often miss the blessings from the process, that is, things which God speaks."

It is clearly the plan and purpose of God for us to go through the wilderness experience. In the wilderness experience you may come to a place where "you hit the wall" many relate to it as though the conscious presence of the Lord seems to have been removed.

A PERSONAL EXAMPLE

I remember when I was saved. For the first few weeks or even months after my surrender to Christ, it was as though I walked on air. Many Christians have described a similar experience. I thought that was the way the Christian life was always going to be. So blissful was my time in the Lord if I had been run over by a Mack Truck I would have blessed the driver as the tires went over me the 4th or 5th time.

If you've lived the Christian life any length of time, you know that the new found euphoria comes to an end. Unfortunately, many churches fail to teach this even though it is a reality in our Christian walk.

We simply will not walk above troubled water for the entirety of our existence in the Lord. There is much we have to learn and our learning can only come through the wilderness experience which includes times of grief and suffering.

Brother Buckingham wrote "Once a man submits his life to God's control, he voluntarily surrenders the right to determine his direction."

When we say "I do" to the Lord, at that moment, even though we may not fully understand all the ramifications of that decision, we begin a journey. That journey is to follow after God with all our heart and to walk in obedience to His perfect will.

Once we give our life over to the Lord the ability to say, "yes" or "no" changes, from that moment we can only say, "yes" if we are to remain in obedience to the Lord. The fact is, He's the boss, because He is God!

It is a matter of complete trust! God knows the direction of our life. He knows the beginning from the end. What the Holy Spirit is desirous of is that Christians learn to follow after the Lord with a willing heart and become conformed to the image of Christ. Through our voluntary surrender we give up our right to self determination. God sets us on a course which will change our lives.

The change comes because we have a new Navigator. The prophet said:

"Behold I will do something new. Now it will spring forth. Will you not be aware of it? I will even make a roadway in the wilderness, rivers in the desert." Isaiah 43:19

It is God's plan and purpose to have those rivers of living water flowing through us. He did not say He would take away the wilderness but He will make a way for us in the middle of the wilderness. The appetite we had for sin changes to an appetite of hunger and thirst for righteousness.

It was quite obvious that the children of Israel needed water and food to sustain them in the natural through their wilderness experience. In the spiritual, we also need sustenance which has been promised by God and is readily found in God's Word and through relationships in His body.

"Spiritual thirst, the need for living water is the dominating factor in the lives of all human beings," said Jamie Buckingham. Man needs "deep water" in the wilderness; we must drink from the rock which is Christ. He is the one who brings forth living water to slack our thirst and give us life. The Bible says those who hunger and thirst after righteousness shall be filled.

A part of what occurs in the wilderness experience, is when we come to the end of the bliss of our blessed experience (though we never lose our salvation), then our feelings begin to change. We sense a lack of the presence or awareness of God. It is at this point that we become hungry and thirsty. God's plan for us then is to seek after the living water, to hunger and thirst after His righteousness.

When we come to this place we should understand that this is normal, that it means it's time for us to drink and it's time for us to eat. Jesus said, "I am the living water" and He also said, that He is the meat that we are to eat (John 6:53). We're to taste and see that

23

the Lord is good and from that experience we begin the process of the transformation of our character so that we can become conformed to the image of Christ. The wilderness experience can be called a place of preparation.

Brother Buckingham wrote: "The wilderness prepares us to become more than a vessel to hold water."

In the wilderness we actually become a source of water for others. It is God's perfect plan that we learn to become our brother's keeper. When everything is given to us, when all of our needs are met, when we're totally dependent upon someone else to feed us and clothe us, we do not learn to care for others.

We often become self absorbed, self centered in the church, thinking that the world revolves around us spiritually. That, my friend, is a baby's mentality. When they're first brought into a family they are the center of attention. They are totally dependent and need total care from others.

God's plan for us is to grow spiritually just as we do in the natural. We are to become more inter-dependent, learning to care one for another. Our focus changes from a life of our own blessing to looking after others and the things that matter to the Lord.

Jamie Buckingham declared, "the only way to reach the promised land is by eating God's diet." In the wilderness if the children of Israel had continued to eat the kind of diet found in Egypt, they would not have survived. There had to be a change to diet that God provided. So it is in your life. If you continue to "eat" the television, party life or any other old world function you won't make it in the wilderness.

There is great grace and mercy for the new Christian. They may still feast on the same old diet as they once did. The thought life hasn't really changed, the mind is not yet renewed. It is a time of grace and mercy and protection from the Lord. But if one is really going to become a young man or a young woman of God who is able to overcome the evil one in preparation to inherit the promises of God, there has to be a change of diet. You must feast on the Word of God, drink of the Holy Spirit and deal with the issues of the heart that keep you blind and from fulfilling your destiny in the Lord.

In this time of change you may even have to change friendships. The friendships of the world become less and less attractive because only true covenant friends are developed during the wilderness experience.

Notice what Jamie Buckingham said, "the character of Moses was a long time in formation. God developed him during his 40 year matriculation at the wilderness university."

God's plan and purpose is to transform us through the crucible of the wilderness. It is in that crucible where we are crushed. It is there that your own desires, needs, hopes and dreams are laid at the foot of the cross; it is there that the new wine of the Holy Spirit begins to come forth from us.

It is only through the crucible of the experience in the wilderness; where we deal with issues of discouragement, depression, sadness and loss; it is only as we face our own lives and the decisions that we make in terms of our relationship with the Lord that true change and transformation occurs.

The Word says:

> "Behold, thou trustest upon the staff of this bruised reed, even upon Egypt, on which if a man lean, it will go into his hand, and pierce it: so is Pharaoh king of Egypt unto all that trust on him." 2 Kings 18:21; (KJV)

> "A bruised reed shall he not break, and smoking flax shall he not quench, till he send forth judgment unto victory." Matthew 12:20; (KJV)

This should make your faith shout... we were never meant to remain in the wilderness where depression, discouragement, and loss dwell. We're all bruised reeds but we have not been forsaken or forgotten. God has provided a city of refugee, a place of hope and healing for all of us. That place is inside the Land of Promise.

In order to prepare yourself for triumphant living you must be toughened spiritually in such a way that you can appropriate the full armor of God. Only then will you be able to stand at battle ready. The toughening process is one that you must be willing to go through. If you are willing to go through it you will learn the lessons that God wants you to learn.

Finally, Jamie Buckingham declares; "the wilderness teaches us that, God is not so interested in rules as He is in relationships."

One of the things that I've experienced is that I draw closer to the Lord and become more intimate with Him in times of trial and trouble. It is during those moments that I feel the Lord's presence personally. After I've cried out to Him, often in pain and anguish, "Lord why am I in this situation? Why am I making the same mistakes all over again? Why can't I fulfill my destiny in you? Why am I always failing?" It is in the midst of the wilderness that God often speaks in the still small voice, "I love you, I am here, I will bless you, I will be your God, you will be My child, trust in Me!"

CHAPTER TWO

Moses In The Wilderness

I've always been intrigued with the life of Moses. What an interesting character, what an intriguing man. He was a man filled with complexities and conflicts and yet obviously chosen by the Lord to be a great deliverer for the people of God.

Although his beginnings were quite humble in the house of his biological parents, Amram and Jochebed, as a baby he was snatched from the river, brought into Pharaoh's court and raised as a son of Pharaoh with all of the luxury and education that position entailed.

After growing up in such an environment and learning the ways of Pharaoh, including leadership, he must have become rather disenchanted. Obviously somewhere along the line Moses became aware that he was an Israelite, he was a Jew, and he was not actually the son of Pharaoh.

Through his disenchantment and disillusionment he recognized and became aware of the needs of his race. God's people were being mistreated, misused and abused by Pharaoh and Pharaoh's men.

Moses, did not understand the timing and purposes of God. When he saw one of his Hebrew brothers in trouble, the Scripture indicates that he took the matter into his own hands, slaying the Egyptian. He thought that his fellow Hebrew would be thankful and honored and would open the doors to his eventual exaltation as a triumphant leader for the people of God.

We know that was God's ultimate plan but God had His own way of accomplishing it. By the world's standards, Moses had been prepared to be a great leader; he had received incredible teaching and training as he was blessed as the son of Pharaoh. But God knows what character must be in the heart before a man or a woman can serve properly in the house of the Lord.

In fear, Moses ran to the back side of the desert, hooking up with his eventual father-in-law, Jethro, where he wandered as a shepherd in the wilderness caring for his father-in-law's sheep, learning the ways of the desert. Of course he had no concept at the time that God's hand was upon him and that he was being prepared to be the deliverer for the people of God.

During his time in the wilderness Moses had a great opportunity to learn about himself. He must have felt terribly rejected, guilty and shameful for having taken the life of the Egyptian. What an incredible blunder.

As the years went by he must have come to a place where he could forgive himself: he certainly was humbled. He was no longer the arrogant son of Pharaoh, but a fugitive, a simple shepherd watching over Jethro's sheep.

In the wilderness he no doubt learned a number of lessons!

He learned to commit himself to Jethro and to understand the whole concept of submission and leadership. Moses became a nobody, if you will, in the desert and yet God was forming something special within him. Jesus the Son of God would later learn obedience through that process.

A new identity was being developed. He learned sensitivity to the needs of the sheep, a sensitivity to their voice, thus developing a compassion for those that were low in spirit or hurting.

I imagine many times Moses would have rehearsed in his mind what he might have done differently if God had given him the opportunity to be more sensitive during the incident with the Egyptian and the Hebrew.

Another interesting thing that Moses learned was how to survive in the desert. He learned by the crucible of experience what it took to survive and thrive in the midst of a great wilderness. He experienced the heat; the need for water. He learned how to find the provisions to sustain life. The desert became so familiar to him that when it came time for true leadership, he was ready with a knowledge of how to exercise it, having acquired empathy and respect for those who were also in the midst of the wilderness. In other words, much of the character of God was being formed in the heart of Moses during his time of wilderness wandering.

At the end of the 40 years, God spoke to Moses from a burning bush. God spoke to Moses of who He was: "*I am that I am have spoken unto you.*" Moses did not assume leadership or presume his capability. In fact he tried to talk God out of it. Who was he? He couldn't speak well. He was no one, a nobody! How could he lead the people of God out of Egypt?

God gave him a staff, a staff of authority. God gave him confidence by allowing him to use His own name: "*I Am that I Am have sent you.*" As a humble servant, he left the wilderness to go to Egypt, no longer speaking as a son of Pharaoh but with the voice of a humble servant, a man of God, a man of faith, a man of power. God miraculously moved through him to lead the children of Israel out of Egypt and into the wilderness.

Once they came out of Egypt, Moses was willing to climb the mountain and receive the Ten Commandments. He was willing to lead when the children of Israel were stubborn, arrogant and disobedient. He did not call down fire from Heaven on the people in arrogance; instead he interceded for them as a shepherd.

He prayed on behalf of the people, "*Oh God, do not punish them for their sins.*" He stood in the gap for them. He had developed a love for the Hebrew people. He was truly a man after God's heart even before David was.

Although Moses was able to see the Promised Land, he was not allowed to enter it. God required perfect obedience from him, but as is often true of great leaders, Moses failed.

At Horeb God gave him the command to strike a rock to obtain water for the people and he obeyed the Word of the Lord. The second time, in the desert of Zin, when God told Moses to speak to a rock to get water for the people he became angry and instead of speaking to the rock he struck it twice. (Num 20:7-12). Water came forth anyway because of the needs of the people, but God needed a model of perfect obedience to be a deliverer, to be a Messiah.

No one is going to be perfectly obedient. Only Jesus was able to do the Father's perfect will at all times. God allowed Moses to look at the Promised Land but he was not permitted to enter it with the children of Israel.

Christian leaders may prepare, develop and work for the kingdom of God, but never see the full results of their work because God's plan is for the continuation of the kingdom through raising up sons and daughters after us. The building of his kingdom often requires us to establish a foundation for others to build upon.

Moses is a type of Christ. His life powerfully demonstrates the need of preparation for ministry, of endurance and strength for the time of wilderness. From his life we can learn much about the wilderness experience. Although Moses as a leader was dynamic, the children of Israel missed out on their opportunity to inherit the promises. The whole generation was lost due to their failure to pass the tests of the wilderness.

There were ten distinct trials the children of Israel faced in the wilderness experience. From these trials, which they failed, we can learn many important character issues God wants us to face and overcome in our journey.

TEN TRIALS IN THE WILDERNESS

Trial Number 1: Fear

The first major trial occurred at the time of the children of Israel's deliverance. The scripture states:

30

"Then the Egyptians chased after him with all the horses and chariots of Pharaoh, his horsemen and his army, and they overtook them camping by the sea, beside Pihahiroth, in front of Baalzephon. And as Pharaoh drew near, the sons of Israel looked, and behold, the Egyptians were marching after them, and they became very frightened; so the sons of Israel cried out to the Lord. Then they said to Moses, 'Is it because there were no graves in Egypt that you have taken us away to die in the wilderness? Why have you dealt with us in this way, bringing us out of Egypt? Is this not the word that we spoke to you in Egypt, saying, leave us alone that we may serve the Egyptians? For it would have been better for us to serve the Egyptians than to die in the wilderness.' But Moses said to the people 'Do not fear! Stand by and see the salvation of the Lord which He will accomplish for you today; for the Egyptians whom you have seen today, you will never see them again forever. The Lord will fight for you while you keep silent.'" Exodus 14:9-14

Trial Number 2: Bitterness

The second major trial, and often the foremost issue to overcome for Christians is bitterness. The Word of God declares:

"And when they came to Marah, they could not drink the waters of Marah, for they were bitter; therefore it was named Marah. So the people grumbled at Moses saying "What shall we drink?" Then he cried out to the Lord, and the Lord showed him a tree; and he threw it into the waters, and the waters became sweet. There he made for them a statute and regulation, and there He tested them. And He said, "If you will give earnest heed to the voice of the Lord your God, and do what is right in His sight, and give ear to His commandments, and keep all His statutes, I will put none of the diseases on you which I have put on the Egyptians; for I, the Lord am your healer. Then they came to Elim where there were twelve springs of water and seventy date palms, and they camped there beside the waters." Exodus 15:23-27

31

All of us have been rejected, abandoned or betrayed at some point in time. This can create a wound and root of bitterness. Old wounds from the past (Egypt), disappointments in the present, including those from Christian leaders, open the door for Satan to seed anger and bitterness that can steal our joy. You have the power not to allow bitterness to enter into your heart.

Notice what the writer of the Book of Hebrews said:

> *"Looking diligently lest any man fail of the grace of God; lest any root of bitterness springing up trouble you, and thereby many be defiled."* Hebrews 12:15 (KJV)

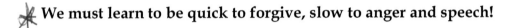 **We must learn to be quick to forgive, slow to anger and speech!**

The Apostle James wrote:

> *"Wherefore, my beloved brethren, let every man be swift to hear, slow to speak, slow to wrath."* James 1:19 (KJV)

Some roots of bitterness and the wounds which caused them may be exceedingly deep and painful but we know that Christ's power is sufficient to set us free, for He bore our sickness and disease, our pains and sorrows on the cross.

Trial Number 3: Hunger

As mentioned previously, you are to hunger and thirst after righteousness. However, when you allow your appetite to go awry, you set yourself up for a time of wandering through the wilderness.

Look at the Words of God to the Children of Israel:

> *"I have heard the grumblings of the sons of Israel; speak to them, saying, 'At twilight you shall eat meat, and in the morning you shall be filled with bread; and you shall know that I am the Lord your God.'" So it came about at evening*

that the quails came up and covered the camp, and in the morning there was a layer of dew around the camp. When the layer of dew evaporated, behold, on the surface of the wilderness there was a fine flake-like thing, fine as the frost on the ground. When the sons of Israel saw it they said to one another, "What is it?" For they did not know what it was. And Moses said to them, "It is the bread which the Lord has given you to eat." This is what the Lord has commanded, "Gather of it every man as much as he should eat; you shall take an omer apiece according to the number of persons each of you has in his tent." And the sons of Israel did so, and some gathered much and some little. When they measured it with an omer, he who had gathered much had no excess, and he who gathered little had no lack; every man gathered as much as he should eat. And Moses said to them, "Let no man leave any of it until morning." But they did not listen to Moses, and some left part of it until morning, and it bred worms and became foul; and Moses was angry with them. And they gathered it morning by morning, every man as much as he should eat; but when the sun grew hot, it would melt. Now it came about in the sixth day they gathered twice as much bread, two omers for each one. When all the leaders of the congregation came and told Moses, then he said to them, "This is what the Lord meant: tomorrow is a Sabbath observance, a holy Sabbath to the Lord. Bake what you will bake and boil what you will boil, and all that is left over put aside to be kept until morning." So they had put it aside to be kept until morning. So they put it aside until morning, as Moses had ordered, and it did not become foul, nor was there any worm in it. And Moses said, "Eat it today, for today is a Sabbath to the Lord; today you will not find it in the field. Six days you shall gather it, but on the seventh day, the Sabbath, there will be none." And it came about on the seventh day that some of the people went out to gather, but they found none. Then the Lord said to Moses, "How long do you refuse to keep My commandments and My instructions? See the Lord has given you the Sabbath; therefore He gives you bread for two days on the sixth day.

Remain every man in his place; let no man go out of his place on the seventh day." So the people rested on the seventh day. And the house of Israel named it manna, and it was like coriander seed, white; and its taste was like wafers with honey." Exodus 16:12-31

God, by His miracle power provided good food for His people, as your spiritual leadership attempts to do for you each week. You are to eat of God's Word daily to remain strong for the journey and to satisfy your hunger for God's goodness.

My friend, from the looks of the Body of Christ, there are many who suffer from eating disorders. Many are unable to absorb much from God's Word on Sunday because they have not eaten from His Word all week. They want to eat but they can't because their stomach has shrunk from not eating.

Trial Number 4: Thirst

Similar to hunger is the thirst for the life of God. Physical thirst can lead you in the wrong direction.

"Therefore, the people quarreled with Moses and said, "Give us water to drink." And Moses said to them, "Why do you quarrel with me? Why do you test the Lord?" But the people thirsted there for water; and they grumbled against Moses and said, "Why, now, have you brought us up from Egypt, to kill us and our children and our livestock with thirst?" So Moses cried out to the Lord, saying, "What shall I do to this people? A little more and they will stone me." Then the Lord said to Moses, "Pass before the people and take with you some of the elders of Israel; and take in your hand your staff with which you struck the Nile, and go." Behold, I will stand before you there on the rock at Horeb; and you shall strike the rock, and water will come out of it, that the people may drink." And Moses did so in the sight of the elders of Israel." Exodus 17:2-6

God wants you to thirst for the water that never runs dry, to thirst for a great flow of His Spirit through your life!

Trial Number 5: Idolatry

If there is a chief of sins, idolatry has to be it. It violates the first commandment! You are to have no other gods before Him. Anything that exalts itself above God can become an idol and must be resisted or torn down.

> *"And it came about, as soon as Moses came near the camp, that he saw the calf and the dancing; and Moses' anger burned, and he threw the tablets from his hands and shattered them at the foot of the mountain. And he took the calf which they had made and burned it with fire, and ground it to powder, and scattered it over the surface of the water, and made the sons of Israel drink it. Then Moses said to Aaron, "What did this people do to you, that you have brought such great sin upon them?" And Aaron said, "Do not let the anger of my lord burn; you know the people yourself, that they are prone to evil. "For they said to me 'Make a god for us who will go before us; for this Moses, the man who brought us up from the land of Egypt, we do not know what has become of him'. And I said to them, 'Whoever has any gold, let them tear it off.' So they gave it to me and I threw it into the fire, and out came this calf."* Exodus 32:19-24

Trial Number 6: Complaining

The children of Israel now had the Law, but were complaining about God. Whether in the Old Testament or today, God's children seem to reserve the "right" to voice their complaints about anything and everything.

The people in the Passages below were complaining against the Lord which is most displeasing. He certainly understands your needs but take note; needless complaining will bring down problems upon you and keep you wandering in the wilderness instead of progressing toward the Promised Land.

> *"Now the people became like those who complain of adversity in the hearing of the Lord; and when the Lord heard it, His anger was kindled, and the fire of the Lord burned among them and consumed some of the outskirts of the camp. The people therefore cried out to Moses, and Moses prayed to the Lord, and the fire died out. So the name of that place was called Taberah, because the fire of the Lord burned among them. And the rabble who were among them had greedy desires; and also the sons of Israel wept again and said, "Who will give us meat to eat? We remember the fish which we used to eat free in Egypt, the cucumbers and the melons and the leeks and the onions and the garlic, but now our appetite is gone. There is nothing at all to look at except this manna. Now the manna was like coriander seed, and its appearance like that of bdellium. The people would go about and gather it and grind it between two millstones or beat it in the mortar, and boil it in the pot and make cakes with it; and its taste was as the taste of cakes baked with oil. And when the dew fell on the camp at night, the manna would fall with it."* Numbers 11:1-9

Trial Number 7: Gluttony

Ouch! One of the sacred cows, excuse the pun, of Christianity is the sin of gluttony. God's desire is for you to do all things in moderation (Philippians 4:5). Anything done in excess can keep you focused on self rather than God.

> *"Now there went forth a wind from the Lord, and it brought quail from the sea, and let them fall beside the camp, about a day's journey on this side and a day's journey on the other side, all around the camp, and about two cubits deep on the surface of the ground. And the people spent all day and all night and all the next day, and gathered the quail (he who gathered least gathered ten homers) and they spread them out for themselves all around the camp."* Numbers 11:31-32

This story also speaks of greed, in an attempt to gather more for yourself than you could ever handle. God blesses you so that you have something to give in time of need. Keep a clear perspective, excess results in a deadly trap.

Trail Number 8: Jealousy or Criticism

Both jealousy and criticism come from the same basic source: **fear and insecurity**!

It is often true that in the midst of temptation and trial, you must guard against becoming overly critical and jealous of others. It is difficult to fully trust God's supply for your needs when this happens. But God is a good God. He is there to care for His children who trust Him.

Aaron and Miriam, out of a spirit of jealousy, spoke out against Moses, the man of God. There were severe consequences for their actions! Sadly this same dangerous practice runs rampant in the Church today! Thankfully, when we sincerely repent, God supplies healing, forgiveness, and restoration just as He did with Aaron and Miriam.

Trial Number 9: Unbelief

After all the tremendous miracles that were done by God through his servant, Moses, you would think that the children of Israel's faith would be high. What a short memory the people had.

> *"Then we set out from Horeb, and went through all that great and terrible wilderness which you saw, on the way to the hill country of the Amorites, just as the Lord our God had commanded us; and we came to Kadesh-barnea. "And I said to you, 'You have come to the hill country of the Amorites which the Lord our God is about to give us. 'See, the Lord your God has placed the land before you; go up, take possession, As the Lord the God of your fathers, has spoken to you. Do not fear or be dismayed'. Then all of you*

approached me and said, 'Let us send men before us, that they may search out the land for us, and bring back to us word of the way by which we should go up, and the cities which we shall enter.' And the thing pleased me and I took twelve of your men, one man for each tribe. "And they turned and went up into the hill country, and came to the valley of Eshcol, and spied it out. Then they took some of the fruit of the land in their hands and brought it down to us: and they brought us back a report and said, 'It is a good land which the Lord our God is about to give us.' "Yet you were not willing to go up, but rebelled against the command of the Lord your God; and you grumbled in your tents and said, 'Because the Lord hates us, He has brought us out of the land of Egypt to deliver us into the hand of the Amorites to destroy us. 'Where can we go up? Our brethren have made our hearts melt, saying, "The people are bigger and taller than we; the cities are large and fortified to heaven. And besides, we saw the sons of the Anakim there.' Then I said to you, 'Do not be shocked, nor fear them. The Lord your God who goes before you will Himself fight on your behalf, just as He did for you in Egypt before your eyes, and in the wilderness where you saw how the Lord your God carried you, just as a man carries his son, in all the way which you have walked, until you came to this place. But for all this, you did not trust the Lord your God, who goes before you on your way, to seek out a place for you to encamp, in fire by night and cloud by day, to show you the way in which you should go. Then the Lord heard the sound of your words and He was angry and took an oath, saying, 'Not one of these men, this evil generation, shall see the good land which I swore to give your fathers, except Caleb the son of Jephunneh; he shall see it, and to him and to his sons I will give the land on which he has set foot, because he has followed the Lord fully.' "The Lord was angry with me also on your account, saying, 'Not even you shall enter there. Joshua the son of Nun, who stands before you, he shall enter there; encourage him, for he will cause Israel to inherit it. Moreover, your little ones who you said would become a prey, and your sons, who this day have no knowledge of good or evil, shall enter there, and I will give it to them, and they shall possess it. But as for you, turn around and set out for the wilderness by the way to the Red Sea'. Then you said to me, 'We have sinned against the Lord; we will indeed go up and fight, just as the Lord our God commanded us. And every man of you girded on his weapons of war and regarded it as easy to go up into the hill country. And the Lord said to me, 'Say to them "Do not go up, nor fight for I am not among you; otherwise you will be defeated before your enemies.' So I spoke to you, but you would not listen. Instead you rebelled against the command of the Lord, and acted presumptuously and went up into the hill country. And the Amorites who lived in that hill country came out against you, and chased you as bees do, and crushed you from Seir to Hormah. Then you returned and wept before the Lord; but the Lord did not listen to your voice, nor give ear to you. So you remained in Kadesh many days, the days that you spent there." Deuteronomy 1:19-46*

Trial Number 10: Trusting God to Enter Cannan

Solomon said in Proverbs 3:5, 6 we must have a simple trust in God.

"Then Joshua rose early in the morning; and he and all the sons of Israel set out from Shittim and came to the Jordan, and they lodged there before they crossed. At the end of three days that the officers went through the midst of the camp; and they commanded the people saying, 'When you see the ark of the covenant of the Lord your God with the Levitical priests carrying it, then you shall set out from your place and go after it." Joshua 3:1-3

The next generation which has been likened to the Joshua generation, will need to put its trust fully in the Lord. His promises are yes! and amen!

Mark my words, He will see you safely into the Land of Promise and help you fulfill your destiny in the Lord… **Trust Him!**

Notice the exactness of God's instructions to the children of Israel as they prepared to cross the Jordan River and enter the Promised Land.

> *"However there shall be between you and it a distance of about 2,000 cubits by measure. Do not come near it that you may know the way by which you shall go, for you have not passed this way before. Then Joshua said to the people, 'Consecrate yourselves, for tomorrow the Lord will do wonders among you.' And Joshua spoke to the priests saying, 'Take up the ark of the covenant and cross over ahead of the people.' So they took up the ark of the covenant and went ahead of the people. Now the Lord said to Joshua, 'This day I will begin to exalt you in the sight of all Israel, that they may know that just as I have been with Moses, I will be with you'. You shall, moreover, command the priests who are carrying the ark of the covenant, saying, 'When you come to the edge of the waters of the Jordan, you shall stand still in the Jordan.' Then Joshua said to the sons of Israel, 'Come here, and hear the words of the Lord your God.' And Joshua said, 'By this you shall know that the living God is among you, and that He will assuredly dispossess from before you the Canaanite, the Hittite, the Hivite, the Perizzite, the Girgashite, the Amorite and the Jebusite. Behold the ark of the covenant of the Lord of all the earth is crossing over ahead of you into the Jordan. Now then, take for yourselves twelve men from the tribes of Israel, one man from each tribe. And it shall come about when the soles of the feet of the priests who carry the ark of the Lord, the Lord of all the earth, shall rest in the waters of the Jordan, the waters of the Jordan shall be cut off, and the waters which are flowing down from above shall stand in one heap."* Joshua 3:4-14

Crossing the river was a giant step of faith for the people who had wandered for forty years in the wilderness. Once they were safely across new challenges faced them!

"Now it came about when Joshua was by Jericho, that he lifted up his eyes and looked and behold, a man was standing opposite him with his sword drawn in his hand, and Joshua went to him and said to him,' Are you for us or for our adversaries?' And he said, 'No, rather I indeed come now as captain of the host of the Lord.' And Joshua fell on his face to the earth, and bowed down, and said to him, 'What has my lord to say to his servant?' And the captain of the Lord's host said to Joshua, 'Remove your sandals from your feet, for the place where you are standing is holy.' And Joshua did so." Joshua 5:13-15

In the New Testament God issues a warning and a promise:

Therefore, holy brethren, partakers of a heavenly calling, consider Jesus, the Apostle and High Priest of our confession. He was faithful to Him who appointed Him, as Moses also was in all His house. For He has been counted worthy of more glory than Moses, by just so much as the builder of the house has more honor than the house. For every house is built by someone, but the builder of all things is God. Now Moses was faithful in all His house as a servant, for a testimony of those things which were to be spoken later; but Christ was faithful as a Son over His house whose house we are, if we hold fast our confidence and the boast of our hope firm until the end. Therefore, just as the Holy Spirit says, "TODAY IF YOU HEAR HIS VOICE, DO NOT HARDEN YOUR HEARTS AS WHEN THEY PROVOKED ME, AS IN THE DAY OF TRIAL IN THE WILDERNESS, WHERE YOUR FATHERS TRIED ME BY TESTING ME AND SAW MY WORKS FOR FORTY YEARS. THEREFORE, I WAS ANGRY WITH THIS GENERATION, AND SAID, "THEY ALWAYS GO ASTRAY IN THEIR HEART; AND THEY DID NOT KNOW MY WAYS"; AS I SWORE IN MY WRATH, "THEY SHALL NOT ENTER MY REST." Take care, brethren, lest there should be in any one of you evil, unbelieving heart, in falling away from the living God. But encourage one another day after day, as long as it is still called "Today", lest any one of you be hardened by the deceitfulness of sin. For we have become partakers of Christ, if we hold fast the beginning of our assurance firm until the end; while it is said, "TODAY IF YOU HEAR HIS VOICE, DO NOT HARDEN YOUR HEARTS, AS WHEN THEY PROVOKED ME." For who provoked Him when they had heard? Indeed, did not all those who came out of Egypt led by Moses? And with whom was He angry for forty years? Was it not with those who sinned, whose bodies fell in the wilderness? And to whom did He swear that they should not enter His rest, but to those who were disobedient? And so we see that they were not able to enter because of unbelief." Hebrews 3:1-19

The warning and the promise continues:

"Therefore let us fear lest, while a promise remains of entering His rest, any one of you should seem to have come short of it. For indeed we have had good news preached to us, just as they also; but the word they heard did not profit them, because it was not united by faith in those who heard. For we who have believed enter that rest, just as He has said, 'AS I SWORE IN MY WRATH, THEY SHALL NOT ENTER MY REST,' although His works were finished from the foundation of the world. For He has thus said somewhere concerning the seventh day, 'AND GOD RESTED ON THE SEVENTH DAY FROM ALL HIS WORKS'; and again in this passage, 'THEY SHALL NOT ENTER MY REST' Since therefore it remains for some to enter it and those who formerly had good news preached to them failed to enter because of disobedience, He again fixes a certain day, 'Today', saying through David after so long a time just as has been said before, 'TODAY IF YOU HEAR HIS VOICE, DO NOT HARDEN YOUR HEARTS.' For if Joshua had given them rest, He would not have spoken of another day after that. There remains therefore a Sabbath rest for the people of God. For the one who has entered His rest has himself also rested from his

works, as God did from His. Let us therefore be diligent to enter that rest, lest anyone fail through following the same example of disobedience. For the word of God is living and active and sharper than any two edged sword, and piercing as far as the division of soul and spirit, of both joints and marrow, and able to judge the thoughts and intentions of the heart. And there is no creature hidden from His sight, but all things are open and laid bare to the eyes of Him with whom we have to do. Since then we have a great high priest who has passed through the heavens, Jesus the Son of God, let us hold fast our confession. For we do not have a high priest who cannot sympathize with our weaknesses, but One who has been tempted in all things as we are, yet without sin. Let us therefore draw near with confidence to the throne of grace, that we may receive mercy and may find grace to help in time of need." Hebrews 4:1-16

God's word is filled with illustrations of His faithfulness in spite of man's failures. He is a God of mercy and second chances (the Prophet Jonah and the Apostle Peter are prime examples).

It would please the Lord if, when faced with trials and temptations in life, you turned to Him in humble obedience and learned the lessons that help you move forward in His will and purpose. Of course this is easier said than done. This is why you need the patterns and processes found in the word of God. These inspire you not to make the same mistakes of those who perished in the wilderness. There is no better model for you or anyone else than Jesus Christ, as seen in The Jesus Experience.

CHAPTER THREE

The Jesus Experience

One of the greatest outpourings of the Spirit in the latter part of the Twentieth Century was the Jesus Movement. It was a tremendous revival that started with the young people of America and spread throughout the world.

Thousands upon thousands confessed Jesus Christ as their Savior on beaches, street corners, subways and coffee houses across the land. Almost any place you found young people you found a new convert testifying about the Lord.

True history will record this move of the Holy Spirit as a miracle outpouring. Many of today's preachers are the product of that mighty visitation. It was during those days that the revelation of having a relationship with Christ through the Holy Spirit was made real.

God's wonderful revelation to the church showed that just as Christ needed to be full of the Holy Spirit so do His followers.

Ask the Holy Spirit to help you grasp the significance of the following Scriptures so that you can apply them to you life!

> *"And Jesus full of the Holy Spirit returned from the Jordan and was led about by the Spirit in the wilderness. For forty days being tempted by the devil and he ate nothing during those days: and when they had ended He became hungry and the devil said to Him, 'If You are the Son of God, tell this stone to become bread.' And Jesus answered him, 'It is written, 'Man shall not live on bread alone' And he (the devil) led Him up and showed Him all the kingdoms of the world in a moment of time and the devil said to Him, I will give You all this domain and its glory, for it's been handed over to me and I give it to whomever I wish. Therefore if You worship before me, it shall all be Yours. And Jesus*

answered and said to him, "It is written, 'You shall worship the Lord your God and serve Him only.' And he led Him to Jerusalem and had Him stand on the pinnacle of the temple and said to Him, 'If You are the Son of God, throw Yourself down from here; for it is written, 'He will give his angels charge concerning You to guard You' and, 'on their hands they will bear You up lest You strike Your foot against a stone.' And Jesus answered and said to him, "It is said, 'You shall not put the Lord your God to the test.' And when the devil had finished every temptation, he departed from him until an opportune time." Luke 4:1-13
which means he came back again

This passage is very significant in the life and ministry of the Lord Jesus Christ. He had been baptized by John and the Father had announced that He was pleased with Him. God had affirmed that Jesus Christ was His own Son.

It was shortly after the blessing and affirmation from His Father that Jesus was led by the Holy Spirit into the wilderness for forty days. This is so important for you to remember; even Jesus had to go through a time of temptation, trial and separation to be released into ministry.

During His wilderness experience the Bible says that He ate nothing. He became hungry just as you and I would be if we fasted forty days. It is during those times, when you are physically hungry, that the devil will try to tempt you with the lust of the flesh, the lust of the eyes and the pride of life as he did with Jesus Christ.

John the Beloved describes these three types of temptation, the lust of the flesh, the lust of the eyes and the pride of life, as something that you and every other child of God experiences. He states that these are not from the Father but from the world. 1 John 2:16

The lust of the flesh is any desire to feed the flesh and satisfy the senses. When Jesus Christ was physically hungry the devil tempted Him to satisfy His flesh by turning stones into bread.

46

Did Jesus have the right and the power to turn the stones into bread? Yes! He definitely did, however, He recognized that His mission in life was to do the will of the Father so He quoted the Scripture: *"It is written, man shall not live on bread alone, But by every word, that proceeds from the mouth of God."* He resisted temptation, rebuked the devil and defeated Satan by using the sword of the Spirit, which is the Word of God.

The devil also tempted Jesus in the lust of the eyes. He took Him to a high mountain and showed Him all the kingdoms of the world in a moment of time.

You may be asking how the devil could do such a thing as that? Remember what Paul the Apostle said of him:

> *"Wherein in time past ye walked according to the course of this world, according to the prince of the power of the air, the spirit that now worketh in the children of disobedience."*
> Ephesians 2:2 KJV

He had the authority to turn the disobedient world over to Jesus Christ if the Lord would only bow down and worship him. Imagine… the devil was trying to tempt the Son of the living God to worship him!

Jesus knew that His Father would crown Him King of kings and Lord of lords, but only after His death and resurrection as planned by the Father from the beginning of the world. So, rather than take the lesser dominion that the devil offered, rather than allowing His eyes to lust after power, He rebuked the devil saying: *"It is written, you shall worship the Lord your God and serve him only."*

Oh, how the devil wanted Jesus to worship him. It would have been the greatest achievement of his sordid existence to have God the Son worship him. That had been his demented desire from the time of his rebellion.

Jesus kept things in proper perspective!

He was willing to wait for the Father's perfect timing to make Him Lord of all rather than yielding to the lust of the eye and accepting momentary pleasure.

Among the devil's devious temptations was the pride of life! Taking the Lord to Jerusalem, he had him stand on the pinnacle of the temple and said:

> "If you are the Son of God, throw Yourself down from here; for it is written, 'HE WILL GIVE HIS ANGELS CHARGE CONCERNING YOU TO GUARD YOU; and, ON their HANDS WILL THEY BEAR YOU UP LEST YOU STRIKE YOUR FOOT AGAINST A STONE."
> Luke 4: 9-11

Our Lord could have taken His rightful place, assumed His place of power and presumptuously accomplished an act for His own benefit out of pride because He was and is the Son of God. But he refused to do anything that could possibly thwart the plan and purpose of God, again He answered, "You shall not put the Lord your God to the test."

The Bible indicates that when Satan finished every temptation he left him until a more opportune time. The devil didn't quit trying to tempt Jesus and to trip him up. He tried to use people and ultimately we know that he believed that through the crucifixion he had won the greatest victory, not realizing that he had completely fallen into the perfect plan of God. When Christ our Savior was crushed, which pleased God according to Isaiah 53, through His death and resurrection your salvation was guaranteed. Jesus Christ became triumphant in His wilderness experience, and so can you.

Immediately after His time of trial and temptation the Bible states that Jesus came forth in great power. It was right after His time in the wilderness that He began to do great miracles. The Word says He went into the synagogue, took the book and read from Isaiah chapter 61:

"The Spirit of the Lord is on me, because He has anointed me to preach good news to the poor. He has sent me to proclaim freedom for the prisoners and recovery of sight for the blind, to release the oppressed, to proclaim the year of the Lord's favor." Luke 4:18, 19

The One who conquered death, hell and the grave announced His true identity...the Messiah!

Another place that is so significant in regards to Jesus' experience of transition is found in the garden of Gethsemane. Jesus, knowing that it was time for His betrayal, knowing that it was time for Him to be crucified, went into the garden with His disciples and prayed, crying out in anguish. Power comes from a crushed life!

He asked the Father if it was possible for the cup to pass from Him, to remove it. Jesus Christ willingly submitted to the purpose and plan of God the Father even though it meant death on the cross. It was on the cross that He took upon Himself the sins of all the world. Mankind's freedom was bought through His ultimate sacrifice.

The pain and grief of the cross paled in comparison to the joy of leading millions into salvation, Hebrews 12:2. He came from the garden in the power of the Holy Spirit. I like especially the account found in the Gospel of John:

"When Jesus had spoken these words he went forth with his disciples over the ravine of the Kidron where there was a garden, into which he himself entered, and his disciples. Now Judas also, who was betraying him, knew the place; for Jesus had often met there with his disciples. Judas then, having received the Roman cohort, and officers from the chief priests and the Pharisees, came there with lanterns and torches and weapons. Jesus, therefore, knowing all the things that were coming upon him, went forth and said to them, 'Whom do you seek?' They answered him, 'Jesus the Nazarene.' He said to them, 'I am He.'" John 18:1-5.

In many versions, the "he" is not actually included. Basically, what Jesus said was, "I Am" and they drew back and fell to the ground.

> "Again, therefore He asked them, 'Whom do you seek?'
> And they said, 'Jesus the Nazarene.' Jesus answered. 'I
> told you that I am He.' If, therefore, you seek Me, let these
> go their way that the word might be fulfilled which He
> spoke 'Of those whom thou hast given me I lost not one.'
> Simon Peter, therefore having a sword, drew it, and struck
> the high priest's slave, and cut off his right ear; and the
> slaves name was Malchus. Jesus therefore said to Peter,
> 'Put the sword into the sheath. The cup which the Father
> has given Me, shall I not drink it?" John 18:7-11

The Bible declares that when Jesus said "I am He", he was clearly identifying himself as, "I am That I Am, speaking to you." When the Lord said this they fell to the ground they were literally knocked down by the power of Jesus' words!

While they were on the ground apparently Peter tried to cut off the head of the high priest but he was not accustomed to using a sword because he missed and hit a servant and cut off his ear. Jesus put the ear back in place and instantly healed him.

Had Jesus not wanted to go with the soldiers, they could not have forced Him. He had the power and authority to withstand them all. Yet, though He had power over man He submitted His will to the Father for your benefit.

In Luke's Gospel we saw that when Jesus had gone through His time of wilderness He came out with great power.

It will be the same for you if you are willing to go through your wilderness experience allowing your heart and life to be transformed by the power of God. Through obedience to God's word, you can come out of your wilderness experience with power and great strength just as Christ did.

CHAPTER FOUR

The Common Cry

Many Christians I have talked to and counseled with over the years have made statements to this effect. "Why does God allow us to go through this wilderness experience? Why can't we just go directly from Egypt to the Promised Land? Why can't we pass go and collect $200 (as in the game of Monopoly), and move into the place where we are able to experience the plan and purpose and power of God?"

This is a cry experienced by all Christians. The cry comes from a common disorder:

✶The battle of the spirit versus the flesh!

To understand this better it will be helpful to review the results of sin as described in the life of the Adam and Eve in the garden of Eden.

> "And they heard the sound of the Lord God walking in the garden in the cool of the day, and the man and his wife hid themselves from the presence of the Lord God among the trees of the garden. Then the Lord God called to the man, and said to him, 'Where are you?' And he said 'I heard the sound of Thee in the garden, and I was afraid because I was naked; so I hid myself.' And He said, 'Who told you that you were naked? Have you eaten from the tree of which I commanded you not to eat.' And the man said, 'The woman whom Thou gavest to be with me, she gave me from the tree, and I ate.' Then the Lord God said to the woman, 'What is this you have done?' And the woman said, 'The serpent deceived me and I ate.' And the Lord God said to the serpent, 'Because you have done this, Cursed are you more than all cattle, And more than every beast of the field; On your belly shall you go, And dust shall you eat All the days of you life; And I will put enmity Between you and

51

the woman, And between your seed and her seed; He shall bruise you on the head And you shall bruise him on the heel.' To the woman He said, 'I will greatly multiply your pain in childbirth, In pain you shall bring forth children; Yet your desire shall be for your husband, And he shall rule over you.' Then to Adam He said, 'Because you have listened to the voice of your wife, and have eaten from the tree about which I commanded you, saying 'You shall not eat from it; Cursed is the ground because of you; in toil you shall eat of it; All the days of your life. Both thorns and thistles it shall grow for you; And you shall eat the plants of the field; By the sweat of your face you shall eat bread, till you return to the ground, Because from it you were taken; For you are dust, And to dust you shall return'. Now the man called his wife's name Eve, because she was the mother of all the living. And the Lord God made garments of skin for Adam and his wife, and clothed them. Then the Lord God said, ' Behold, the man has become like one of us, knowing good and evil; and now, lest he stretch out his hand, and take also from the tree of life, and eat, and live forever'- therefore the Lord God sent him out from the garden of Eden, to cultivate the ground from which he was taken. So He drove the man out; and at the east of the garden of Eden He stationed the cherubim, and the flaming sword which turned every direction, to guard the way to the tree of life. Now the man had relations with his wife Eve, and she conceived and gave birth to Cain, and she said, "I have gotten a manchild with the help of the Lord." And again she gave birth to his brother Abel. And Abel was a keeper of flocks, but Cain was a tiller of the ground. So it came about in the course of time that Cain brought an offering to the Lord of the fruit of the ground. And Abel, on his part also brought of the firstlings of his flock and of their fat portions. And the Lord had regard for Abel and for his offering; but for Cain and for his offering He had no regard. So Cain became very angry and his countenance fell. Then the Lord said to Cain, 'Why are you angry? And why has your countenance fallen? If you do well will not your countenance be lifted up? And if you do not do well, *sin is crouching at the door; and its desire is for you but you must master it'. And Cain told Abel his brother. And it came about when they were in the field, that Cain rose up against Abel his brother and killed him. Then the Lord said to Cain, 'Where is Abel your brother?' And he said, 'I do not know. Am I my brother's keeper?'"* Genesis 3:8- 4:9

We know that the woman was deceived by the enemy, and the man chose to disobey God, thus a curse was placed upon the world with eternal consequences. We will not take time to look at all the curses but will simply review some of them.

Death entered into the existence of man, including spiritual death. Man's spirit is dead without Christ. Ephesians 2:3, says that the unregenerate are children of wrath by nature. Their father, the devil, is the father of all lies.

As a result of the fall, man's nature became distorted, disturbed and distraught. Due to sin, mankind's soul, mind, will and emotions become separated from the magnificent knowledge of God.

The first man and woman were created with absolutely brilliant minds. They were able to name and to rule all of the animal kingdom, the birds of the air and the fish of the sea. Ha-adam, the original Hebrew word means both Adam and Eve. Both ruled and reigned over all of God's creation.

They were very clever but as a result of Adam's fall the mind of man became twisted and distorted and no longer understood God and His ways. Man cannot find God on his own.

What does this mean?

Before the fall, Adam's choices were simple, whatever God wanted that is what Adam did. So he walked in perfect harmony with his Father. Then he made a wrong choice!

53

One of the common difficulties you face in this age is that you have multiple choices. That's one of the effects of the fall. You have so many different paths you can choose from and if you lack the knowledge of God, all too often, you make wrong choices. God created you with a brilliant mind but you must depend on His leadership or you will fail miserably.

This world is dominated by the negative!

Most people view the world not from a glass half full but half empty.

Even if you were raised in a family system where you were affirmed, loved, blessed, and given a sense that your future was filled with hope and accomplishment, if you are not careful you will tend to be dominated by negative emotions. That's a result of the fall.

Even your body, your physical shell, suffers from the fall. Physical suffering, disease, and disorders (none of which are from God) are result from the fall of man. You are subject to the foibles of the flesh and of your sinful nature.

One of the results of sin is rejection. Mankind was rejected by God! You have no doubt experienced significant rejections in Your life. Man by nature has a desperate need to belong to something or someone.

Most have lived in Egypt, (the world), and attempt to adapt to Egypt or to the lifestyle of sin. You may choose to belong to the world system so that people will like and accept you. Unfortunately, that doesn't work. It never did and it never will because the world has nothing to give that will ultimately provide health and satisfaction.

Tremendous guilt and shame came upon man through the fall!

When we recognize how far short we've fallen from the plan and purpose of God, that indeed all have sinned and fallen short of the glory of God, (Rom. 3:23) we recognize that we all have a need to reclaim our sense of self worth.

Most of us have tried in many ways to build up our esteem ourselves and to bolster our sagging ego.

You may have tried power, position, prestige, via greed. You may have tried to develop relationships that give you self-esteem and make you feel worthwhile, to help you overcome the guilt and shame experienced because of sin.

Keith Miller in his book, *Sin, The Ultimate Addiction*, speaks of that very thing. Everyone is addicted to something. Addiction to sin is what must be faced, whether it's acted out in drugs or alcohol or workaholicism or avoidism or whatever other ism there may be; every human being suffers guilt and shame because of the fall.

Finally when you suffer from weakness and helplessness it is normal to try gathering strength by using self control. The sad fact is, anyone trying to control their world eventually recognizes how out of control the world really is.

It's only in Christ that you and I have hope!

When we come to know Him and walk the pathway of righteousness, we are able to begin the process of overcoming a sense of rejection, guilt, shame and helplessness. We must recognize that "in Christ" we are accepted; we are adopted children. We've been adopted into the family of God; we were personally chosen by God Himself.

Grasp this truth and hold on to it! He is your Father, and He loves you! No longer will you experience guilt and shame. You know you have worth because the Father has said you matter to Him. He sent his only begotten Son to die on the cross for you.

John 3:16 speaks volumes regarding your worth to God!

In your weakness and helplessness you gain strength as you give up control. Notice what the Bible says:

> *"Trust in the Lord with all your heart, lean not on your own understanding; in all our ways acknowledge him, and he will make your paths straight."* Proverbs 3:5-6

This Scripture declares unequivocally that God has a plan for your life. The control and strength is in God. In spite of the affects of the fall God's plan through Jesus is to bring about complete healing and restoration.

Within your salvation experience is a process of growth and change. At first you have the wonderful sense of being accepted and free from sin. You know you are accepted, free from guilt and shame and you are strong in the Lord.

But there's an internal battle that the Apostle Paul wrote about that deals with the issues of the flesh. Don't be discouraged or defeated when the issues of the flesh eventually emerge. *Amen*

Here is what Paul said:

> *"Or do you not know, brethren (for I am speaking to those who know the law), that the law has jurisdiction over a person as long as he lives? For the married woman is bound by law to her husband while he is living; but if her husband dies, she is released from the law concerning the husband. So then if, while her husband is living, she is joined to another man, she shall be called an adulteress; but if her husband dies, she is free from the law, so that she is not an adulteress, though she is joined to another man. Therefore, my brethren, you also were made to die to the Law through the body of Christ, that you might be joined to another, to Him who was raised from the dead, that we might bear fruit for God. For while we were in the flesh, the sinful passions, which were aroused by the Law, were at work in the members of our body to bear fruit for death. But now we*

have been released from the Law, having died to that by which we were bound, so that we serve in newness of the Spirit and not in the oldness of the letter. What shall we say then? Is the Law sin? May it never be! On the contrary, I would not have come to know sin except through the Law; for I would not have known about coveting if the Law had not said, 'YOU SHALL NOT COVET.' But sin, taking opportunity through the commandment, produced in me coveting of every kind; for apart from the Law sin is dead. And I was once alive apart from the Law; but when the commandment came, sin became alive, and I died; and this commandment, which was to result in life, proved to result in death for me; for sin, taking opportunity through the commandment, deceived me, and through it killed me. So then, the Law is holy, and the commandment is holy and righteous and good. Therefore did that which is good become a cause of death for me? May it never be! Rather it was sin, in order that it might be shown to be sin by effecting my death through that which is good, that through the commandment sin might become utterly sinful. For we know that the Law is spiritual; but I am of flesh, sold into bondage to sin. For that which I am doing, I do not understand; for I am not practicing what I would like to do, but I am doing the very thing I hate. But if I do the very thing I do not wish to do, I agree with the Law, confessing that it is good. So now, no longer am I the one doing it, but the sin which indwells me. For I know that nothing good dwells in me, that is, in my flesh; for the wishing is present in me, but the doing of the good is not. For the good that I wish, I do not do; but I practice the very evil that I do not wish. But if I am doing the very thing I do not wish, I am no longer the one doing it, but sin which dwells in me. I find then the principle that evil is present in me, the one who wishes to do good. For I joyfully concur with the law of God in the inner man, but I see a different law in the members of my body, waging war against the law of my mind, and making me a prisoner of the law of sin which is in my members. Wretched man that I am! Who will set me *free from the body of this death? Thanks be to God through Jesus Christ our Lord! So then, on the one hand I myself with my mind am serving the law of God, but on the other, with my flesh the law of sin."* Romans 7:1-25

The fleshly individual is a person who lives according to the dictates of the flesh or their own desires (1 Corinthians 3:3). It is important that you understand this concept because you are dualistic in many ways.

A war is raging in you between the flesh and the spirit. It is a part of the wilderness experience as designed by God to deal with the flesh in such a way that the Spirit of God eventually fully manifests Himself within you. This makes it possible for you to inherit the promises and to recapture what was lost in the fall.

You have been born of God! You were created in His image, you are to have dominion and purpose in His divine Kingdom. The flesh, as seen in Romans 8:8, has ingrained habit patterns that appeal to your mind and tell you that you should, could, and can live independently of God. This is your flesh!

When you attempt to set yourself up as the ruler of your own life your body can experience many disorders. Tension, anxiety, stress, and diseases, are prime examples! Another example of living in and for your flesh is double-mindedness. James says that a double-minded man is unstable in all his ways.

As you enter the wilderness you may no longer sense that perfect peace of the Lord and you may begin to desire the old life which will create an internal struggle.

You may question, "Do I really want to live for God, or do I want to return to Egypt and the old lifestyle?" This instability within your mind can lead to instability in your emotions or your heart.

While traversing the wilderness you may display a gamut of emotions ranging from fear, to anxiety, to anger and hurt. It is possible to respond very childishly, even explosively or become filled with despair and resentment.

In the crucible of the wilderness, when trials and temptations come, all types of things may come out of your heart. Emotional responses, which have been buried, or denied may come to the surface. In fact, many of these rediscovered conflicts though forgiven have not been fully repented of. This can be due to ignorance or lack of teaching, or a denial of the truth. Often, these issues were under the surface until God knew you were ready to deal with them with the help of the Holy Spirit.

Take note of this important truth, your free will becomes disabled through sin, which means that you must choose to walk after the flesh, or after the Spirit. Paul said:

> *"But I say, walk by the Spirit, and you will not carry out the desire of the flesh. For the flesh sets its desire against the Spirit, and the Spirit against the flesh; for these are in opposition to one another, so that you may not do the things that you please. But if you are led by the Spirit, you are not under the Law."* Galatians 5:16-18

When the flesh life becomes dominant, it is usually manifested in the crucible of the wilderness experience. Your spirit, which is alive in Christ, can become quenched. (Romans 8:9 and 1 Thessalonians 5:19). You may lose spiritual vitality and your desire to serve God can wane. You may even question if you are saved. Let me assure you, when you are in the wilderness you are saved. Since God is working something out in your life, cooperate with what the Holy Spirit is doing.

You will find a dramatic change beginning to occur but you must be willing to submit to the process of change that we will outline in great detail later in this book.

Do not become disenchanted or discouraged about your time in the wilderness. As millions before you would attest, you will make it.

With the help of your discipler and the Holy Spirit, you will be ready to enter into the promises of God in rapid fashion.

CHAPTER FIVE

Character Development

Webster defines character as "a mark, letter, figure, sign, stamp, any distinctive mark, an essential feature, nature, the total of qualities making up an individual, moral excellence, a person noted for eccentricity, a personage in a play or novel. To depict particular qualities, to distinguish, to give character or characteristic."

Character, is the totality of any individual's life. As developed over time it's a mixture of a person's temperament, i.e., the innate tendencies, the personality or the interaction of the environment, family, school, church, etc. on the individual temperament.

Character is something that is clearly seen by those who know someone. God's desire for every believer is that they grow and become mature in Him. Simply stated, character growth is the putting on of the new man which we will look at a little later (Ephesians 4:24).

In order to understand character and how character develops, we will take some pictures from the natural world of human behavior. Most psychologists say that much of an individual's character is formed by ages 5-7. The basic style in which we see ourselves, our self image, our view of the world, goodness or badness, our basic way of approaching life and people, is fairly well established at least by age 10.

Who we are in relationship to others is fairly readily seen by this age. Our character very rarely changes without some sort of powerful intervention into a person's life after the formative years. Our character is under girded by the habits that we learn in our daily existence.

God has created us so marvelously!

We have a portion of our brain called **the autonomic nervous**

system which governs our physical activity. That is, we are governed by habit patterns, patterns that make us feel comfortable. Human behavioral research has established that it takes approximately 30-40 days to break an old habit and 30-40 days to establish a new one.

A simple example of that might be helpful here.

You may be interested in changing your eating habits for weight loss or for health purposes. To do so after doing some reading and becoming educated on the topic, you need to start a new way of eating while simultaneously stopping the old way of eating, and do so for approximately 30-40 days in order to establish this new healthier style of eating as a habit. During the process of habituation or of making something a habit in one's life, there are a couple of stages that we go through.

The initial stage of a change usually brings about a certain amount of exhilaration. You have noticed that starting the diet can be difficult, but once you make the decision to do it the first few days are usually quite pleasant. You may have a few minor battles and temptations, but for the most part you continue to move forward in your resolve to change without great difficulty.

But beware, somewhere around the 20th day of the change you may experience some intense anxiety.

One of the things about humanity is that we fear change. Change is painful and uncomfortable so it is normal to avoid changes because they upset our applecart. Thus the closer you get to the actual 30-40 day mark the greater the anxiety will be, the greater the difficulty, and most likely you will sabotage your own growth.

However, if you get past the 40 day mark successfully, what you will find is that a new habit is put into place and the new habit makes you feel comfortable. So comfortable in fact, that if you change the habit again by attempting to go back to the old ways of doing things you will feel uncomfortable.

This is why discipline, learning to read the Word, pray and fellowship on a regular basis is so important. As you do this consistently it tends to develop positive habits that will bless and strengthen you and carry you through difficult times in life. Character formation is simply a series of learned patterns in many different areas of your life that make you feel comfortable. In truth, many of your old patterns, learned in the world, are no longer positive or helpful but are quite problematic.

CHAPTER SIX

Character Formed and Deformed

How is character fully formed? Character is formed in the crucible of day to day life. You learn how to respond based on how your family of origin, the church and society taught you. You incorporate those teachings into a matrix of habits that carry you over a lifetime.

The Bible speaks of the need for us to be conformed to the very image of God's Son, the Lord Jesus Christ (Romans 8:29).

In Antioc, the disciples were first called Christians. Even though it was meant as a term of derision it was taken as a badge of honor in that the Christians recognized the life of Christ within them.

The Bible says that if any man be in Christ he is a new creation, old things pass away, behold all things become new (2 Corinthians 5:17). This is what Paul is saying: The moment you are born again your spirit becomes alive. You are a newly created individual.

From God's viewpoint all of your old life is completely gone and you are a brand new creation in Him.

That is an absolute reality and yet there is a second reality that you must deal with!

Paul talked about it in Romans 7. To paraphrase his words: "The things that I love to do, I do not seem to do; the things I don't want to do I always seem to do." But notice the apostle didn't stop there, he said: "It is not I, it is not the real me but it is sin or the flesh nature in me, my old life which has been developed through time. The old nature still hangs around to plague me."

That's why the Apostle Paul wrote in Romans 12, Ephesians 4 and in other places, about the need to deal with the old self.

Character becomes deformed because of the sin nature. Deformed character is the epitome of sin being acted out in the flesh. God wants to transform your character through a process of the renewing of the mind, which includes putting off the old, renewing the mind, and putting on the new.

Character is deformed because of sin. Satan's strategy is to keep you locked into an attitude that you can never become all that God created you to be. He wants you to believe the delusions of the past and to desire the old life, rather then go through the process of change, which is necessary if you are to fulfill your destiny in God.

So... how is character transformed?

CHAPTER SEVEN

Character Transformed

Let's see what the Apostle Paul has to say about character transformation.

He wrote:

> *"I urge you therefore, brethren, by the mercies of God that you present your bodies a living and holy sacrifice, acceptable to God which is your spiritual service of worship. And do not be conformed to this world, but be transformed by the renewing of your mind, that you may prove what the will of God is, that which is good and acceptable and perfect."* Romans 12:1-2

In my book, *Journey to Wholeness: Restoration of the Soul*, I speak a great deal about the process of renewing the mind. Rather than go into detail what I have already written, let me state here some of the more important components found in this Scripture.

First, Paul taught the church in Rome that they needed to come to a place of presenting themselves fully and completely to God which was reasonable and a part of their spiritual service to the Lord, part of their worship.

This was undoubtedly a problem in that day for the apostle to mention it. There must have been Christians who did not want to come to the Light through worship, instead they would withhold areas of their lives from the Lord which created darkness within.

In the second verse it says, do not be conformed to this world. That statement is a positive statement but there's also a negative aspect to it. That is, it must be possible to be conformed or to live life as a fleshly Christian. That is certainly not the will of God. His will is for you to be transformed!

You are not to be conformed to the world any longer. You are not to be bound as a slave to your old lifestyle as you once were!

The word transformed is from the word *metamorphosis*. It is the term used to describe the change that takes place when a caterpillar turns into a butterfly; changing from one type to another.

Next is the renewing of your mind. You do this by presenting your mind to the Lord. Humble yourself before him and allow the Word of God to go deep within so that you are transformed at the very core of your being.

Remember, God's Word is like a mirror. When you look into it intently, it will read your heart and change it as you obey its principles.

The Apostle James wrote the same thing when he said that you should no longer delude yourself but that you must *"put aside all filthiness and all that remains of wickedness, so that in humility you might receive the word implanted, which is able to save (transform) your soul"* James 1:21.

What the servant of the Lord is saying to the Hebrew believers is that it is quite possible for them to still have filthiness and wickedness in their heart. They must be willing to humble themselves, present their bodies and themselves to the Lord to receive the word implanted.

The word "implanted" there speaks of being literally pounded in, meditated on so that you understand it, but even more than understanding, to have revelation of the meaning of the word. In this way you come under the power of the word, because when it is implanted in you, it is able to save your soul.

James is not talking about initial salvation; rather, he is talking about the continuing progressive work of sanctification in your life. It's vitally important that you understand God's plan will bring you all the way to a fully transformed character so that you actually

68

function according to God's perfect plan.

My premise is that transformation occurs in the time of the wilderness experience. When you humbly submit your heart to the Lord you become able to prove what is the will of God; that which is His good will, His acceptable will, even His perfect will.

The Scripture that speaks best about transformation through the church community is discussed in the book of Ephesians.

Let's discuss those verses!

The Apostle Paul wrote to born-again, Spirit filled believers who were saved through the local church in the city of Ephesus, one of the most powerful churches of that day.

He so eloquently stated that you do not learn Christ through a hard heart, in sensuality or in ignorance, and that you should no longer walk in old sinful patterns. God's plan is for you to continue to move forward in your spiritual life.

In reference to your former manner of life or to your fleshly nature, he said, lay aside the old self, put off the old man which is being corrupted in accordance with the lust of deceit. Ephesians 4:17-21

The lust of deceit is lies that you desire to be true!

The Bible says that you will be corrupted or torn down if you hold on to un-Biblical beliefs. The Lord wants you to put all of those aside. You do that by speaking them out, by confessing them, and going through a process of change which we will talk about in the second part of this book and in your personal 40 Days Journal.

The Apostle Paul said to be renewed in the spirit of your mind or in the center of your being, in your heart. Your mind must be renewed by the *"washing of water with the word."* Ephesians 5:26

Finally the Word says:

"Put on the new self which in the likeness of God, has been created in righteousness and holiness of the truth." Ephesians 4:24

Character growth is right living combined with right thinking. It is the putting on of the new man. "Putting on," is accomplished in the same way as "putting off" through the confession of your mouth and believing in your heart.

God's plan for the church, to be transformed through this wonderful process!

It is important to remember that character development, change and transformation is not just for the pastor, although according to 1 Timothy chapter 3, a minister, an elder or deacon will be disqualified if their character has not been transformed to a place of maturity.

The development of character is for all believers because as the Scripture says:

"Now then we are ambassadors for Christ, as though God did beseech you by us: we pray you in Christ's stead, be ye reconciled to God." 2 Corinthians 5:20 (NKJ)

The Apostle Peter said:

"We are a royal priesthood, a holy nation." 1 Peter 2:9

You must be willing to go through the process of transformation and change in order to fully become what God intended you to be!

CHAPTER EIGHT

Steps To Character Change

The most important step that any Christian can take, and it needs to be a daily experience is to submit yourself to the Lord in humble obedience as the Lord of your life.

I still remember the first time I prayed and asked the Lord that if there was anything in my heart, anything in my character that needed to be changed to please reveal it to me.

Every day since then I pray this simple prayer, "Lord I submit myself to You. You are my Father, my Lord, my King. I am your servant. I pray that you will change me, mold me, and use me, for the sake of Your Kingdom."

I promise you… the Lord hears prayers like that!

It was at that time, as described in my book, *I Want To Be Like You Dad*, that God began to expose some real, deep, seedy, rotten, nasty parts of my heart. As He did initially I wanted to run or blame others for the problems which surfaced. Ultimately, I had to recognize that I was the problem, I needed to change, I needed to grow up in godliness and mature in Him.

The process or the steps for character change begin with the willingness to admit your weakness or inability to change yourself and then submit to the Word of God.

These are the instructions from the Lord:

> *"Is anyone among you suffering? Let him pray. Is anyone cheerful? Let him sing praises. Is anyone among you sick? Let him call for the elders of the church, and let them pray over him, anointing him with oil in the name of the Lord; and the prayer offered in faith will restore the one who is sick, and the Lord will raise him up, and if he has*

committed sins, they will be forgiven him. Therefore, confess your sins to one another, and pray for one another, so that you may be healed. The effective prayer of a righteous man can accomplish much." James 5:13-16

In this chapter, the Apostle James, speaking to the church, primarily the Hebrew church, beginning with the 13th verse says, *"Is any among you suffering? Let him pray."* One thing is certain, if you are in your wilderness time, you are going to experience suffering.

It is not a time to shout and not a time to run, neither is it a time to go back to Egypt, although there will be a temptation to do all of those things; but more importantly, it's a time to pray. Ultimately healing prayer, prayer of confession, prayer of deliverance is what will bring about the transformation in our character.

The apostle also wrote, *"Is any among you cheerful? Let him sing praises."* Hopefully the people around you won't be singing praises when you're in a time of suffering. But if you are cheerful, sing and rejoice in the Lord.

Verse 14 says, *"Is anyone among you sick? Let him call for the elders of the church."* The word sickness there can mean more then just physical sickness, it includes sickness of the soul. James said, *"Call for the elders of the church,"* who is to do the calling? The one who is sick!

It's not up to the elders, the mature ones, to determine who is sick and to hunt them down. You must be willing to submit yourself to the process of change. You are to call the elders and let them pray over you; anoint you with oil in the name of the Lord. The prayer offered in faith will restore and the Lord will raise you up. If sin has caused the sickness, it will be forgiven you.

When you look at the issues of character in your life and realize the results of sin, sometimes sins that you have committed, and sometimes sins that have been committed against you, it is easy to become discouraged.

You may exclaim, "How could God love someone like me, I am such a failure!" Regardless of your feelings, you need to confess your sins and faults and repent. Remember the meaning of true repentance is to change your thinking; this in turn will change your lifestyle.

God provides forgiveness and cleansing but you must be willing to accept the healing prayer!

James continued by writing, *"therefore, confess your sins one to another."*

Many people think that since the Word said, "Confess your sins one to another that they can confess to anybody." Perhaps a rabbi or a priest thinking they will keep it confidential. That may be true, but they probably will not be able to pray powerfully or effectively. Ultimately there is a linkage between "one another" and the elders listed in verse 14.

We are to confess to someone who is mature in the Lord, who has gone through a process of growth and change. This does not mean that they are perfect by any means but that they understand, empathize, and care.

Again, verse 16 says to confess your sins to one another and pray for one another so that you may be healed. That healing process includes restoration. You become whole and complete in the Lord.

The effective prayer of a righteous man could accomplish much. I very much like the King James version where it says, *"the fervent and effectual prayer of a righteous man availeth much."*

Most of us who are involved in charismatic churches are very good at fervency; but we're not always very good at effectiveness. We can only be effective, which means to pray to the mark, if we know what the situation really is.

A part of the 40 day program presented in the next section, is designed to reveal the areas of your life that desperately needs prayer... prayer for deliverance... for cleansing and for healing. As you cooperate in the process and allow the Holy Spirit to reveal the areas of your character that need change, and as you pray especially as seen in Matthew 18:19 a prayer of agreement, the power of God will be released on your behalf.

What's an effective prayer? A prayer that's prayed to the mark!

The Holy Spirit has been birthing the concept of the 40 days to the promise in my heart for many, many years.

I recognize that I didn't go through a systematic process, I wish I had. Instead of systematically dealing with the issues of my heart, putting off the old and renewing my mind, putting on the new, I've done my process as most Christians do, hit-or-miss.

I didn't understand what was happening to me when I first "hit the wall" with this experience. I've taken many trips around the mountain, as it were, not walking in obedience or faithfulness and I've fallen into sin and suffered the consequences.

Usually, not always, I have failed out of ignorance. I've cried out to God so many times, "Lord help me, deliver me, set me free from my bondage," never really understanding what it takes, what it means, or how to do it.

I wish I could have had someone who loved me, and understood the process. Someone who understood God's plan and could have walked me through my 40 days. I honestly believe I would have come to a place of maturity much sooner.

I must say I have learned a great deal in my wilderness wandering. Not the kind of lessons I like to speak about and not the kind that really please God.

Some lessons create shame, remorse, anxiety, anger, and sadness and will keep you from fulfilling your true destiny in the Lord. I pray that you will take the next step by reviewing the 40 steps and begin the process, the 40 days to your promise, so that you might receive all that God has in store for you.

Matt 18:19
James 5:13-16

CHAPTER NINE

Issues Of The Heart

I mentioned in the introduction of how God revealed to me the strategy for going through the wilderness. One of the things that He spoke to me, which was very strange to me at the time, was that if I would take the time to search His word, He would reveal to me the 20 areas of the old nature that need to be "put off" in a person's life. These are areas that need to be set aside, confessed, and repented of.

He also promised that I would discover the 20 areas of an individual's heart that need to be "put on" and established foundationally.

The Lord told me that if I would search the Scriptures I would find these 20 negative and 20 positive characteristics and that through a process of reviewing them, praying over them and facing the truth, tremendous growth and change would occur in people's lives.

In this section we will look at the issues of the heart, the positive and the negative, that dualistic part of us, the deeds of the flesh versus the fruit of the Spirit. Taking in the whole counsel of God from the fullness of the Bible we will see these as common characteristics in individual's lives.

These need to be uncovered and removed so that you can be set free to become all that God wants you to be.

In Jeremiah 17:9 the Bible says that *"The heart is deceitful and desperately wicked above all things: who can know it?"*

Jeremiah was speaking about the natural heart or better yet the mind, the seat of man's affections not the spiritual person, that is, those who have been born again.

By the Spirit, as I mentioned before, from 2 Corinthians 5:17, you become a brand new creation. Your spirit is alive but your soul which has been damaged by the old nature, by sin, the fall, and by your own wrong choices, still continues to plague you and must be dealt with. That's why there's a need for continuing progressive sanctification or cleansing and healing and restoration of your heart.

If a man's heart is changed, his behavior will be different!

It's amazing how many people, even Christians, think about one of the most important decisions in their life, that is, the choosing of a spouse, in a haphazard way. They will allow themselves to be led by their passion, not by the Holy Spirit, not even by their minds.

It is easy to be attracted to someone who will fulfill your negative expectations. That is, they will reinforce your belief in the way marriage and family life is supposed to be. What a frightening thought, especially if your expectations are based solely on your images from your family of origin!

Even if you had the best of all parents you're going to have a distorted view from God's perspective. Thus, you must deal with the heart from the renewed position. It is vitally important to deal with the issues of heart and character, so that our renewed mind will override our heart, and allow us to make right choices.

God has revealed to me 20 negative and 20 positive characteristics of the heart or the mind or the seat of your affections.

I want you to review them, study them, and hopefully as you prayerfully read through the Scriptures that apply to each characteristic of the heart you will be taught a simple process that when applied with a helper, can begin the process of mending the issues of your heart.

Let me say again there comes a time and a season for change. If you're reading this book as a leader, I trust you are reading it with the hope of being able to apply the principles found here to your own life as well as to the lives of those to whom you minister.

Pray for wisdom and guidance to recognize when an individual is in a time of change and transition. It is during that time that you are able to apply these divine principles and lead them to complete victory. If they are not prepared spiritually to go through the 40 Day process, it will not have the same effect as if one applies it in the timing of the Lord.

Only the Holy Spirit knows the right time. It won't be 40 days after salvation for most people, or 40 weeks, 40 months or 40 years, it comes in the fullness of time when God is ready. So part of your preparation is to pray and believe that the Holy Spirit will reveal to you, as well as to those to whom you minister, when it's their time and season for change.

If you have taught new converts about the 40 day process, they'll be willing to say, "Hey pastor, hey teacher, hey prophet, I think my time has come." At that moment you can help them start the process which is ordained by God and which will bring about a true transformation of character.

In the next chapter you will discover the 20 negative characteristics of the heart that need to be laid aside, confessed and repented of before the Lord.

CHAPTER TEN

The 20 Old

CAUTION! Just because a certain type of sin is listed here it does not mean that you specifically suffer from the results of this kind of sin. These are the issues that can plague the heart of any man or any woman. It may or may not apply to you. In either case, it doesn't hurt to learn about it.

We're going to look at this list of sins in the order given to me by the Lord. However, they can be done in any order that the Holy Spirit reveals to you. People who have had a background of witchcraft may want to deal with that first. Perhaps you need to deal with hatred or disobedience or one of the other areas of sin first. In all things, be sensitive to the Holy Spirit as you go through the process.

The goal is to do one a day, in your daily devotions. My recommendation is to have a minimum of 1/2 hour every day for 40 days. You need to set aside time either in the morning or the evening. It needs to be a consistent time devoted to the process of change.

Everyday you will read, discuss and pray through one of the "20 old" followed by one of the "20 new." You will be going through the process twice. You may ask, why twice? Think of your heart, your mind like an onion. We must remove things one layer at a time.

If you go through it once, it may not affect you deeply. The second time you process through these characteristics the Word will impact you at a much deeper level. Again, the goal is to do more than a spiritual exercise. It is to develop a new habit of daily devotion, of confession of sin and dealing with issues in your life before they become a major problem.

Following is a list of 20 negative characteristics which covers a majority of the issues of the heart.

The old habits:

IMMORALITY(

HYPOCRISY ν

IDOLATRY 3 (stubborness)

WITCHCRAFT 4 (rebellion)

HATRED 5

STRIFE 6

CONTENTIOUSNESS 7

SEDITIONS 8

HERESIES 9

JEALOUSY 10

REVELING $)1$

IDLENESS $)2$

MALICE $)3$

ANXIETY $)4$

PRIDE $)5$

CRITICISM $)6$

DISOBEDIENCE $)7$

REBELLION $)8$

LYING $)9$

WRATH 20

We're going to look at each one briefly, listing the various Scriptures that go along with each of these negative characteristics of the heart.

82

IMMORALITY

The first one listed is immorality. Immorality can be a sexual sin, either past or present. The Greek word is *Porneia*. Certainly the Bible teaches us not to lust or fornicate. In Scripture lust means more than just to think about someone sexually but to think on them as though to desire and to possess them as an object.

Any form of sexual behavior that treats an individual as an objects rather than a person is sexual immorality. According to the Bible it can also be listed as laviciousness or lust in general.

You will want to look up these verses and write them out for yourself so that you can pray and deal with the issues involved. In your personal diary or journal write your thoughts and general impressions after each major portion of scripture.

Malachi 2:15b
"So guard yourself in your spirit, and do not break faith with the wife of your youth."

Matthew 5:27
"You have heard that it was said, 'Do not commit adultery'."

John 8:3
"The teachers of the law and the Pharisees brought in a woman caught in adultery."

Matthew 19:4
"Haven't you read, he replied, 'that at the beginning the Creator made them male and female.'"

Romans 7:3
"So then if, while her husband is living, she is joined to another man she shall be called an adulteress; but if her husband dies, she is free from the law, so that she is not an adulteress, though she is joined to another man."

1 Corinthians 6:9-10a
"Or do you not know that the unrighteous shall not inherit the kingdom of God? Do not be deceived; neither fornicators, nor idolaters, nor adulterers, nor effeminate, nor homosexuals,...shall inherit the kingdom of God."

2 Peter 2:14
"...having eyes full of adultery and that never cease from sin, enticing unstable souls, having a heart trained in greed, accursed children;..."

Also under **lust or fornication**:

1 Corinthians 5:1
"It is actually reported that there is immorality among you, and immorality of such a kind as does not exist even among the Gentiles, that someone has his father's wife."

1 Corinthians 6:18
"Flee immorality. Every other sin that a man commits is outside the body, but the immoral man sins against his own body."

1 Corinthians 7:2
"But because of immoralities, let each man have his own wife, and let each woman have her own husband."

1 Corinthians 10:8
"Nor let us act immorally, as some of them did, and twenty three thousand fell in one day."

Ephesians 5:3
"But do not let immorality or any impurity or greed even be named among you, as is proper among saints;..."

Colossians 3:5
"Therefore consider the members of your earthly body as dead to immorality, impurity, passion, evil desire, and greed, which amounts to idolatry."

1 Thessalonians 4:3
"For this is the will of God, your sanctification; that is, that you abstain

from sexual immorality."

Lasciviousness:

Romans 1:27
"...and in the same way also the men abandoned the natural function of the woman and burned in their desire toward one another, men with men committing indecent acts and receiving in their own persons the due penalty of their error. "

2 Corinthians 12:21
"I am afraid that when I come again my God may humiliate me before you, and I may mourn over many of those who have sinned in the past and not repented of the impurity, immorality and sensuality which they have practiced."

Ephesians 4:19
"And they having become callous, have given themselves over to sensuality, for the practice of every kind of impurity with greediness."

Jude 1:7
"Just as Sodom and Gomorrah and the cities around them, since they in the same way as these indulged in gross immorality and went after strange flesh, are exhibited as an example, in undergoing the punishment of eternal fire."

Lust:

Proverbs 6:25
"Do not desire her beauty in your heart, Nor let her catch you with her eyelids."

Matthew 5:28
"But I say to you, that everyone who looks on a woman to lust for her has committed adultery with her in his heart."

Romans 13:9
"The commandments, 'Do not commit adultery,' 'Do not murder,' 'Do not steal,' 'Do not covet,' and whatever other commandment there may be

are summed up in this one rule: 'Love your neighbor as yourself.'"

Galatians 5:16
"But I say, walk by the Spirit, and you will not carry out the desire of the flesh."

Colossians 3:5
"Therefore consider the members of your earthly body as dead to immorality, impurity, passion, evil desire, and greed, which amounts to idolatry. "

1 Thessalonians 4:5
"Not in passionate lust like the heathen, who do not know God;…"

2 Timothy 2:22
"Now flee from youthful lusts, and pursue righteousness, faith, love and peace, with those who call on the Lord from a pure heart."

James 1:15
"Then when lust has conceived, it gives birth to sin; and when sin is accomplished, it brings forth death."

1 Peter 2:11
"Beloved, I urge you as aliens and strangers to abstain from fleshly lusts, which wage war against the soul."

Again, I suggest that you read every Passage listed. If you are processing someone through the "40 Days to the Promise" or you are going through it yourself, it is a necessity that you read each verse. As you read it ask the Holy Spirit if this is an issue in your life. If it is, during the next chapter you will learn how to deal with it through a time of healing prayer.

HYPOCRISY

Hypocrisy is essentially judging someone harshly and not judging yourself with an equal measure. Several Scriptures speak about hypocrisy. It is an issue that is especially problematic. Jesus Christ consistently called the Pharisees and Sadducees hypocrites because they were religious but their hearts were not right with God.

Study these Scriptures:

Proverbs 26:20-28
"For lack of wood the fire goes out, and where there is no whisperer, contention quiets down. Like charcoal to hot embers and wood to fire, so is a contentious man to kindle strife. The words of a whisperer are like dainty morsels, and they go down into the innermost parts of the body. Like an earthen vessel overlaid with silver dross are burning lips and a wicked heart. He who hates disguises it with his lips, but he lays up deceit in his heart. When he speaks graciously, do not believe him, for there are seven abominations in his heart. Though his hatred covers itself with guile, his wickedness will be revealed before the assembly."

Luke 6:42
"Or how can you say to your brother, 'Brother, let me take out the speck that is in your eye,' when you yourself do not see the log that is in your own eye? You hypocrite, first take the log out of your own eye, and then you will see clearly to take out the speck that is in your brother's eye."

Luke 12:1
"Under these circumstances, after so many thousands of the multitude had gathered together that they were stepping on one another, He began saying to His disciples first of all, 'Beware of the leaven of the Pharisees, which is hypocrisy.'"

Luke 12:2
"But there is nothing covered up that will not be revealed, and hidden that will not be known."

Luke 12:54-59
"And He was also saying to the multitudes, "When you see a cloud rising in the west, immediately you say, 'A shower is coming,' and so it turns out. And when you see a south wind blowing, you say, 'It will be a hot day,' and it turns out that way. You hypocrites! You know how to analyze the appearance of the earth and the sky, but why do you not analyze this present time? And why do you not even on your own initiative judge what is right? For while you are going with your opponent to appear

before the magistrate, on your way there make an effort to settle with him, in order that he may not drag you before the judge, and the judge turn you over to the constable, and the constable throw you into prison. I say to you, you shall not get out of there until you have paid every last cent."

Luke 13:10-17
"And He was teaching in one of the synagogues on the Sabbath. And behold, there was a woman who for eighteen years had had a sickness caused by a spirit; and she was bent double, and could not straighten up at all. And when Jesus saw her, He called her over and said to her, 'Woman, you are freed from your sickness.' And He laid His hands upon her; and immediately she was made erect again, and began glorifying God. And the synagogue official, indignant because Jesus had healed on the Sabbath, began saying to the multitude in response, 'There are six days in which work should be done; therefore come during them and get healed, and not on the Sabbath day.' But the Lord answered him and said, 'You hypocrites, does not each of you on the Sabbath untie his ox or his donkey from the stall, and lead him away to water him? And this woman, a daughter of Abraham as she is, whom Satan has bound for eighteen long years, should she not have been released from this bond on the Sabbath day?' And as He said this, all His opponents were being humiliated; and the entire multitude was rejoicing over all the glorious things being done by Him."

Luke 6:46-49
"Why do you call Me, 'Lord, Lord, 'and do not do what I say? I will show you what he is like who comes to me and hears my words and puts them into practice. He is like a man building a house, who dug down deep and laid the foundation on rock. When a flood came, the torrent struck the house but could not shake it, because it was well built. But the one who hears my words and does not put them into practice is like a man who built a house on the ground without a foundation. The moment the torrent struck that house, it collapsed and its destruction was complete."

Romans 16:17
"Now I urge you brethren, keep your eye on those who cause dissensions and hindrances contrary to the teaching which you learned, and turn away from them."

Romans 2:1
"Therefore you are without excuse, every one of you who passes judgment, for in that you judge another, you condemn yourself; for you who judge practice the same things. "

Romans 2:21-22
"You, therefore who teach another, do you not teach yourself? You who preach that one should not steal, do you steal? You who say that one should not commit adultery, do you commit adultery? You who abhor idols, do you rob temples?"

Romans 16:18
"For such men are slaves, not of our Lord Christ but of their own appetites; and by their smooth and flattering speech they deceive the hearts of the unsuspecting."

1 Timothy 4:2
"...by means of the hypocrisy of liars seared in their own conscience as with a branding iron,..."

Titus 1:16
"They profess to know God, but by their deeds they deny Him, being detestable and disobedient, and worthless for any good deed."

James 3:8-18
"But no one can tame the tongue; it is a restless evil and full of deadly poison. With it we bless our Lord and Father; and with it we curse men, who have been made in the likeness of God; from the same mouth come both blessing and cursing. My brethren, these things ought not to be this way. Does a fountain send out from the same opening both fresh and bitter water? Can a fig tree, my brethren, produce olives, or a vine produce figs? Neither can salt water produce fresh. Who among you is wise and understanding? Let him show by his good behavior his deeds in the gentleness of wisdom. But if you have bitter jealousy and selfish ambition in your heart, do not be arrogant and so lie against the truth. This wisdom is not that which comes down from above, but is earthly, natural, demonic. For where jealousy and selfish ambition exist, there is disorder and every evil thing. But the wisdom from above is first pure, then peaceable, gentle, reasonable, full of mercy, and good fruits unwavering, without hypocrisy.

And the seed whose fruit is righteousness is sown in peace by those who make peace."

Hypocrisy is something that must be dealt with. You have no right to judge anyone unless you have first dealt with the issues in your own heart.

IDOLATRY

Idolatry is the lifting up or the placing of anything, whether an object, person, a title, or vision, ahead of God.

The Bible demands that we put away all idols. Therefore if we have anything, including a relationship, a husband, a wife, a job, or whatever, that we give priority to above God, is an idol. Remember… God is a jealous God and He will have no other gods before Him. To have His best in your life you must put them away.

The Scriptures that refer to this include:

Genesis 35:1-4
"Then God said to Jacob, "Arise, go up to Bethel, and live there; and make an altar there to God, who appeared to you when you fled from brother, Esau." So Jacob said to his household and to all who were with him, "Put away the foreign gods which are among you, and purify yourselves, and change your garments; and let us arise and go up to Bethel; and I will make an altar there to God, who answered me in the day of my distress, and has been with me wherever I have gone." So they gave to Jacob all the foreign gods which they had, and the rings which were in their ears; and Jacob hid them under the oak which was near Shechem."

Exodus 20:1-5
"Then God spoke all these words, saying, "I am the Lord your God, who brought you out of the land of Egypt, out of the house of slavery. You shall have no other gods before Me. You shall not make for yourself an idol, or any likeness of what is in heaven above or on the earth beneath, or in the water under the earth. You shall not worship them or serve them; for I, the Lord your God, am a jealous God, visiting the iniquity of the fathers on the children, on the third and the fourth generations of those who hate

Me."

Deuteronomy 7:25
"The graven images of their gods you are to burn with fire; you shall not covet the silver or the gold that is on them, nor take it for yourselves, lest you be snared by it, for it is an abomination to the Lord your God."

Joshua 24:13-15
"(God says) ...'And I gave you a land on which you had not labored, and cities which you had not built, and you have lived in them; you are eating of vineyards and olive groves which you did not plant.' "Now, therefore, fear the Lord and serve Him in sincerity and truth; and put away the gods which your fathers served beyond the River and in Egypt, and serve the Lord. And if it is disagreeable in your sight to serve the Lord, choose for yourselves today whom you will serve: whether the gods which your fathers served which were beyond the River, or the gods of the Amorites in whose land you are living; but as for me and my house we will serve the Lord."

1 Samuel 7:3
"Then Samuel spoke to all the house of Israel, saying, "If you return to the Lord with all your heart, remove the foreign gods and the Ashtaroth from among you and direct your hearts to the Lord and serve Him alone; and He will deliver you from the hand of the Philistines."

2 Kings 3:2
"And he did evil in the sight of the Lord, though not like his father and his mother; for he put away the sacred pillar of Baal which his father had made."

2 Kings 23:21-25
"Then the king commanded all the people saying, "Celebrate the Passover to the Lord your God as it is written in this book of the covenant."

1 Chronicles 15:1-8
"Now David built houses for himself in the city of David; and he prepared a place for the ark of God, and pitched a tent for it. Then David said, "No one is to carry the ark of God but the Levites; for the Lord chose them to carry the ark of God, and to minister to Him forever." And David

assembled all Israel at Jerusalem, to bring up the ark of the Lord to its place, which he had prepared for it. And David gathered together the sons of Aaron, and the Levites: of the sons of Kohath, Uriel the chief, and 120 of his relatives; of the sons of Merari, Asaiah the chief, and 220 of his relatives; of the sons of Gershom, Joel the chief, and 130 of his relatives; of the sons of Elizaphan, Shemaiah the chief, and 200 of his relatives."

Isaiah 42:8
"I am the LORD; that is my name! I will not give My glory to another nor My praise to graven images."

Jeremiah 10:1-6
"Hear what the LORD says to you, O house of Israel. This is what the LORD says: "Do not learn the ways of the nations or be terrified by signs in the sky, though the nations are terrified by them. For the customs of the peoples are worthless; they cut a tree out of the forest, and a craftsman shapes it with his chisel. They adorn it with silver and gold; they fasten it with hammer and nails so it will not totter. Like a scarecrow in a melon patch, their idols cannot speak; they must be carried because they cannot walk. Do not fear them; they can do no harm nor can they do any good." No one is like you, O LORD; you are great, and your name is mighty in power."

Acts 17:29
"Therefore since we are God's offspring, we should not think that the divine being is like gold or silver or stone - an image made by man's design and skill."

Romans 1:21-32
"For although they knew God, they neither glorified him as God nor gave thanks to him, but their thinking became futile and their foolish hearts were darkened. Although they claimed to be wise, they became fools and exchanged the glory of the immortal God for images made to look like mortal man and birds and animals and reptiles. Therefore God gave them over in the sinful desires of their hearts to sexual impurity for the degrading of their bodies with one another. They exchanged the truth of God for a lie, and worshiped and served created things rather than the Creator - who is forever praised. Amen. Because of this, God gave them over to shameful lusts. Even their women exchanged natural relations for

unnatural ones. In the same way the men also abandoned natural relations with women and were inflamed with lust for one another. Men committed indecent acts with other men, and received in themselves the due penalty for their perversion. Furthermore, since they did not think it worthwhile to retain the knowledge of God, he gave them over to a depraved mind, to do what ought not to be done. They have become filled with every kind of wickedness, evil, greed and depravity. They are full of envy, murder, strife, deceit and malice. They are gossips, slanderers, God-haters, insolent, arrogant and boastful; they invent ways of doing evil; they disobey their parents; They are senseless, faithless, heart-less, ruthless. Although they know God's righteous decree that those who do such things deserve death, they not only continue to do these very things but also approve of those who practice them."

1 John 5:21
"Dear children, keep yourselves from idols."

In order to please the Lord and grow in your walk with him, it is necessary to root out sins that you have depended upon for comfort in the past.

WITCHCRAFT

Number four is witchcraft or the occult. There is much written about witchcraft and the occult. It is any kind of behavior that you dabble with that is satanic in nature. It includes magic, necromancy, sorcery or things of like nature. Any attempt to contact the dead or to bring worship toward the devil will most certainly bring a curse upon your life and affect your heart.

It's important to deal with the occult from a Biblical standpoint. Let me share with you the Scriptures that speak of witchcraft in its various forms. There are a number of them.

Genesis 44:15
"Joseph said to them, "What is this you have done? Don't you know that a man like me can find things out by divination?"

Numbers 22:7
"The elders of Moab and Midian left, taking with them the fee for divination. When they came to Balaam, they told him what Balak had said."

Deuteronomy 18:14
"The nations you will dispossess listen to those who practice sorcery or divination. But as for you, the LORD your God has not permitted you to do so."

1 Samuel 6:2
The Philistines called for the priests and the diviners and said, "What shall we do with the ark of the LORD? Tell us how we should send it back to its place."

Jeremiah 27:9
"So do not listen to your prophets, your diviners, your interpreters of dreams, your mediums or your sorcerers who tell you, 'You will not serve the king of Babylon.'"

Ezekiel 13:23
"Therefore you will no longer see false visions or practice divination. I will save my people from your hands. And then you will know that I am the LORD."

Ezekiel 21:21
"For the king of Babylon will stop at the fork in the road, at the junction of the two roads, to seek an omen: He will cast lots with arrows, he will consult his idols, he will examine the liver."

Zechariah 10:2
"The idols speak deceit, diviners see visions that lie; they tell dreams that are false, they give comfort in vain. Therefore the people wander like sheep oppressed for lack of a shepherd."

Acts 16:16
"Once when we were going to the place of prayer, we were met by a slave girl who had a spirit by which she predicted the future. She earned a great deal of money for her owners by fortune-telling."

Magicians:

Genesis 41:24
"The thin heads of grain swallowed up the seven good heads. I told this to the magicians, but none could explain it to me."

Exodus 7:11
"Pharaoh then summoned wise men and sorcerers, and the Egyptian magicians also did the same things by their secret arts:"

Exodus 8:19
"The magicians said to Pharaoh, "This is the finger of God." But Pharaoh's heart was hard and he would not listen, just as the LORD had said."

Exodus 9:11
"The magicians could not stand before Moses because of the boils that were on them and on all the Egyptians."

Daniel 2:2
"So the king summoned the magicians, enchanters, sorcerers and astrologers to tell him what he had dreamed."

Daniel 4:7
"When the magicians, enchanters, astrologers and diviners came, I told them the dream, but they could not interpret it for me."

Necromancy, which is defined as trying to determine the future by contacting the spirits of the dead:

Deuteronomy 18:10-12 (KJV)
"There shall not be found among you any one that maketh his son or his daughter to pass through the fire, or that useth divination, or an observer of times, or an enchanter, or a witch, Or a charmer, or a consulter with familiar spirits, or a wizard, or a necromancer. For all that do these things are an abomination unto the LORD: and because of these abominations the LORD thy God doth drive them out from before thee."

1 Samuel 28:11
"Then the woman asked, "Whom shall I bring up for you?" 'Bring up Samuel,' he said."

Isaiah 8:19
"When men tell you to consult mediums and spiritists, who whisper and mutter, should not a people inquire of their God? Why consult the dead on behalf of the living?"

Soothsayers which are similar to necromancy;

Isaiah 2:6
"You have abandoned your people, the house of Jacob. They are full of superstitions from the East; they practice divination like the Philistines and clasp hands with pagans."

Micah 5:12
"I will destroy your witchcraft and you will no longer cast spells."

Sorcery:

Deuteronomy 18:10
"Let no one be found among you who sacrifices his son or daughter in the fire, who practices divination or sorcery, interprets omens, engages in witchcraft,…"

2 Kings 17:17
"They sacrificed their sons and daughters in the fire. They practiced divination and sorcery and sold themselves to do evil in the eyes of the LORD, provoking him to anger."

2 Kings 21:6
"He sacrificed his own son in the fire, practiced sorcery and divination, and consulted mediums and spiritists. He did much evil in the eyes of the LORD, provoking him to anger."

Isaiah 47:9
"Both of these will overtake you in a moment, on a single day: loss of children and widowhood. They will come upon you in full measure, in

spite of your many sorceries and all your potent spells."

Malachi 3:5
"So I will come near to you for judgment. I will be quick to testify against sorcerers, adulterers and perjurers, against those who defraud laborers of their wages, who oppress the widows and the fatherless, and deprive aliens of justice, but do not fear me," says the LORD Almighty."

Acts 8:9-11 (KJV)
"But there was a certain man, called Simon, which beforetime in the same city used sorcery, and bewitched the people of Samaria, giving out that himself was some great one: To whom they all gave heed, from the least to the greatest, saying, This man is the great power of God. And to him they had regard, because that of long time he had bewitched them with sorceries."

Acts 13:6
"They traveled through the whole island until they came to Paphos. There they met a Jewish sorcerer and false prophet named Bar-Jesus."

Revelation 18:23
"The light of a lamp will never shine in you again. The voice of bridegroom and bride will never be heard in you again. Your merchants were the world's great men. By your magic spell all the nations were led astray."

Revelation 21:8
"But the cowardly, the unbelieving, the vile, the murderers, the sexually immoral, those who practice magic arts, the idolaters and all liars--their place will be in the fiery lake of burning sulfur. This is the second death."

Under **witchcraft** specifically we have:

Exodus 22:18
"Do not allow a sorceress to live."

Leviticus 19:31
"Do not turn to mediums or seek out spiritists, for you will be defiled by them. I am the LORD your God."

1 Samuel 15:23
"For rebellion is like the sin of divination, and arrogance like the evil of idolatry. Because you have rejected the word of the LORD, he has rejected you as king."

1 Samuel 28:7
"Saul then said to his attendants, "Find me a woman who is a medium, so I may go and inquire of her." "There is one in Endor," they said."

1 Chronicles 10:13
"Saul died because he was unfaithful to the LORD; he did not keep the word of the LORD and even consulted a medium for guidance."

Isaiah 8:19
"When men tell you to consult mediums and spiritists, who whisper and mutter, should not a people inquire of their God? Why consult the dead on behalf of the living?"

Isaiah 19:3
"The Egyptians will lose heart, and I will bring their plans to nothing; they will consult the idols and the spirits of the dead, the mediums and the spiritists."

Micah 5:12
"I will destroy your witchcraft and you will no longer cast spells."

Gal 5:19-21 (KJV)
"Now the works of the flesh are manifest, which are these; Adultery, fornication, un-cleanness, lasciviousness, idolatry, witchcraft, hatred, variance, emulations, wrath, strife, seditions, heresies, envyings, murders, drunkenness, revellings, and such like: of the which I tell you before, as I have also told you in time past, that they which do such things shall not inherit the kingdom of God."

Also **lying wonders** can be seen as a part of, or caused by, witchcraft:

Exodus 7:11
"Pharaoh then summoned wise men and sorcerers, and the Egyptian

magicians also did the same things by their secret arts…"

Exodus 7:22
"But the Egyptian magicians did the same things by their secret arts, and Pharaoh's heart became hard; he would not listen to Moses and Aaron, just as the LORD had said."

Exodus 8:7
"But the magicians did the same things by their secret arts; they also made frogs come up on the land of Egypt."

Matthew 7:22
"Many will say to me on that day, 'Lord, Lord, did we not prophesy in your name, and in your name drive out demons and perform many miracles?' "

Matthew 24:24
"For false Christs and false prophets will appear and perform great signs and miracles to deceive even the elect - if that were possible."

2 Thessalonians 2:9
"The coming of the lawless one will be in accordance with the work of Satan displayed in all kinds of counterfeit miracles, signs and wonders,…"

Revelation 13:13
"And he performed great and miraculous signs, even causing fire to come down from heaven to earth in full view of men."

Revelation 13:14
"Because of the signs he was given power to do on behalf of the first beast, he deceived the inhabitants of the earth. He ordered them to set up an image in honor of the beast who was wounded by the sword and yet lived."

Revelation 16:14
"They are spirits of demons performing miraculous signs, and they go out to the kings of the whole world, to gather them for the battle on the great day of God Almighty."

Revelation 19:20

"But the beast was captured, and with him the false prophet who had performed the miraculous signs on his behalf. With these signs he had deluded those who had received the mark of the beast and worshiped his image. The two of them were thrown alive into the fiery lake of burning sulfur."

Any contact with witchcraft in the past needs to be confessed and repented of. There are times that actual deliverance of demonic forces must occur. That's another reason why working with someone who is mature in the Lord is very, very helpful.

HATRED:

Number five is hatred. Hatred is holding anger, resentment and bitterness against someone. It was deemed by Jesus to be equivalent to murder.

The Scriptures include:

Leviticus 19:17

"Do not hate your brother in your heart. Rebuke your neighbor frankly so you will not share in his guilt."

Proverbs 10:12

"Hatred stirs up dissension, but love covers over all wrongs."

Proverbs 15:17

"Better a meal of vegetables where there is love than a fattened calf with hatred."

John 7:7

"The world cannot hate you, but it hates me because I testify that what it does is evil."

John 15:18

"If the world hates you, keep in mind that it hated me first."

John 15:25
"But this is to fulfill what is written in their Law: 'They hated me without reason.'"

1 John 2:9
"Anyone who claims to be in the light but hates his brother is still in the darkness."

1 John 2:11
"But whoever hates his brother is in the darkness and walks around in the darkness; he does not know where he is going, because the darkness has blinded him."

1 John 3:15
"Anyone who hates his brother is a murderer, and you know that no murderer has eternal life in him."

1 John 4:20
"If anyone says, "I love God," yet hates his brother, he is a liar. For anyone who does not love his brother, whom he has seen, cannot love God, whom he has not seen."

In reference to **murder**:

Exodus 1:16
"When you help the Hebrew women in childbirth and observe them on the delivery stool, if it is a boy, kill him; but if it is a girl, let her live."

Exodus 20:13
"You shall not murder."

Proverbs 28:17
"A man tormented by the guilt of murder will be a fugitive till death; let no one support him."

Matthew 2:16
"When Herod realized that he had been outwitted by the Magi, he was furious, and he gave orders to kill all the boys in Bethlehem and its vicinity who were two years old and under, in accordance with the time he

had learned from the Magi."

Matthew 19:18
"Jesus replied, 'Do not murder, do not commit adultery, do not steal, do not give false testimony',…"

Acts 7:19
"He dealt treacherously with our people and oppressed our forefathers by forcing them to throw out their newborn babies so that they would die."

Romans 13:9
"The commandments, "Do not commit adultery," "Do not murder," "Do not steal," "Do not covet," and whatever other commandment there may be, are summed up in this one rule: "Love your neighbor as yourself."

1 Peter 4:15
"If you suffer, it should not be as a murderer or thief or any other kind of criminal, or even as a meddler."

If you are holding any hatred or bitterness against anyone now or from the past it is vitally important to ask the Holy Spirit to reveal it to you! If you are, you must confess it to the Lord. You may need to make restitution and seek forgiveness from the party that the hatred has been held against.

In all cases, you need to check with someone who is mature in the Lord because there are times when confession of such a thing can cause more pain to the individual to whom you are confessing it.

Make sure you do everything according to the law of love. Is it going to be a blessing, or could your action cause additional problems in someone else's life?

STRIFE:

Strife can be simply described as someone who likes to cause conflict. There are people who enjoy stirring up strife. They like to get people to argue and fight with each other. The Bible doesn't talk so much about strife as it does about what causes strife. Such as:

Proverbs 13:10 (Pride)
"*Pride only breeds quarrels, but wisdom is found in those who take advice.*"

Proverbs 26:21 (Contentiousness)
"*As charcoal to embers and as wood to fire, so is a quarrelsome man for kindling strife.*"

Proverbs 29:22 (Anger)
"*An angry man stirs up dissension, and a hot-tempered one commits many sins.*"

1 Timothy 6:4
"*He is conceited and understands nothing. He has an unhealthy interest in controversies and quarrels about words that result in envy, strife, malicious talk, evil suspicions.*"

James 3:16
"*For where you have envy and selfish ambition, there you find disorder and every evil practice.*"

If you are the one who enjoys stirring up strife then it is an issue of your heart that needs to be dealt with. There's usually a reason for it. Whether you seek attention that way or if it's the way you get revenge, it's something that you must look at and face, confess and turn from it.

CONTENTIOUSNESS:

Number 7 is contentiousness or a contentious spirit. To be contentious means to be quarrelsome. It is similar to strife. It is a person who likes to have arguments or quarrels. There are intellectuals who spend their whole life arguing. They consider it intellectual to debate. Jesus said, "let your yea be yea and your nay be nay." Anything more than that may come from a contentious spirit.

The Scriptures that go along with this include:

Psalm 140:1-3 (KJV)
"To the chief Musician, A Psalm of David. "Deliver me, O LORD, from the evil man: preserve me from the violent man; Which imagine mischiefs in their heart; continually are they gathered together for war. They have sharpened their tongues like a serpent; adders' poison is under their lips. Selah."

Proverbs 15:18
"A hot-tempered man stirs up dissension, but a patient man calms a quarrel."

Proverbs 17:19
"He who loves a quarrel loves sin; he who builds a high gate invites destruction."

Proverbs 18:6
"A fool's lips bring him strife, and his mouth invites a beating."

Proverbs 26:21
"As charcoal to embers and as wood to fire, so is a quarrelsome man for kindling strife."

Habakkuk 1:3
"Why do you make me look at injustice? Why do you tolerate wrong? Destruction and violence are before me; there is strife, and conflict abounds."

SEDITIONS:

Number 8 is called seditions, which is another word for gossip. Gossip causes many problems. The Apostle James spoke of the tongue as being a raging fire, especially when gossip is being spread and seditions are actively being shared.

The Scriptures that go along with this:

Proverbs 6:2
"...you have been trapped by what you said, ensnared by the words of your mouth,..."

Proverbs 10:18
"He who conceals his hatred has lying lips, and whoever spreads slander is a fool."

2 Thessalonians 3:11
"We hear that some among you are idle. They are not busy; they are busybodies."

1 Timothy 5:13
"Besides, they get into the habit of being idle and going about from house to house. And not only do they become idlers, but also gossips and busybodies, saying things they ought not to."

1 Peter 4:15
"If you suffer, it should not be as a murderer or thief or any other kind of criminal, or even as a meddler."

If you are involved in gossip, you need to stop immediately! Start by confessing that you are guilty of this sin. Gossip, means saying things about people with a malicious intent. It is a raging fire from hell.

HERESIES:

Number 9 is heresies or influences. Heresies can be defined as an opinion that's contrary to orthodox opinion and teaching or belief.

Some people would rather believe a radical teaching or follow after evil influences than believe the Truth. If you have trouble believing the truth or you tend to want to believe the influences of evil, this is an area of your heart that needs cleansing.

The Scriptures regarding this include:

2 Chronicles 21:6
"He walked in the ways of the kings of Israel, as the house of Ahab had done, for he married a daughter of Ahab. He did evil in the eyes of the LORD."

Jeremiah 23:15
"Therefore, this is what the LORD Almighty says concerning the prophets: "I will make them eat bitter food and drink poisoned water, because from the prophets of Jerusalem ungodliness has spread throughout the land."

Mark 15:11
"But the chief priests stirred up the crowd to have Pilate release Barabbas instead."

Acts 13:8
"But Elymas the sorcerer (for that is what his name means) opposed them and tried to turn the proconsul from the faith."

Romans 2:24
"As it is written: "God's name is blasphemed among the Gentiles because of you."

Romans 14:15
"If your brother is distressed because of what you eat, you are no longer acting in love. Do not by your eating destroy your brother for whom Christ died."

1 Corinthians 5:6
"Your boasting is not good. Don't you know that a little yeast works through the whole batch of dough?"

1 Corinthians 8:10
"For if anyone with a weak conscience sees you who have this knowledge eating in an idol's temple, won't he be emboldened to eat what has been sacrificed to idols?"

Galatians 5:9
"A little yeast works through the whole batch of dough."

JEALOUSY:

Number 10 is jealousy. Jealousy is a fear of losing something you believe you deserve. To envy is to want or covet something. This is a grave problem especially in materialistic America. You need to recognize that you are to desire spiritual gifts and seek the Kingdom of God but you are not to envy or live a life of jealousy.

If you have jealousy in your heart it is not from the Lord. It needs to be dealt with by confession, repentance, forgiveness and healing.

The Scriptures relating to jealousy are:

Genesis 37:4 (Regarding Joseph)
"When his brothers saw that their father loved him more than any of them, they hated him and could not speak a kind word to him."

Exodus 20:5
"You shall not bow down to them or worship them; for I, the LORD your God, am a jealous God, punishing the children for the sin of the fathers to the third and fourth generation of those who hate me,…"

Exodus 34:14
"Do not worship any other god, for the LORD, whose name is Jealous (one who permits no rivals), is a jealous God."

Joshua 24:19
"Joshua said to the people, 'You are not able to serve the LORD. He is a holy God; he is a jealous God. He will not forgive your rebellion and your sins'."

Judges 8:1
"Now the Ephraimites asked Gideon, 'Why have you treated us like this? Why didn't you call us when you went to fight Midian?' And they criticized him sharply."

1 Samuel 18:8
"Saul was very angry; this refrain galled him. "They have credited David with tens of thousands," he thought, "but me with only thousands. What

more can he get but the kingdom? "

1 Kings 15:22
"Then King Asa issued an order to all Judah--no one was exempt--and they carried away from Ramah the stones and timber Baasha had been using there. With them King Asa built up Geba in Benjamin, and also Mizpah."

Proverbs 6:34
"For jealousy arouses a husband's fury, and he will show no mercy when he takes revenge."

Matthew 20:12
"'These men who were hired last worked only one hour,' they said, 'and you have made them equal to us who have borne the burden of the work and the heat of the day.'"

Luke 15:28 (Regarding the prodigal son).
"The older brother became angry and refused to go in. So his father went out and pleaded with him."

1 Corinthians 10:22
"Are we trying to arouse the Lord's jealousy? Are we stronger than he?"

REVELING:

Number 11 is reveling.

Reveling is defined by Webster to mean, to make merry, or to carouse, or if you will, a party spirit. You find your whole thought life revolves around the desire to live a party life. If your attitude towards life has become eat, drink and be merry, your heart needs to change. The person with this heart attitude is like the person who wanted to return to Egypt, to eat the leeks and garlics, or to have the old life of bondage. It is an issue of the heart more than it is of behavior, and requires the touch of God.

Exodus 32:6
"So the next day the people rose early and sacrificed burnt offerings and

presented fellowship offerings. Afterward they sat down to eat and drink and got up to indulge in revelry."

Judges 9:27
"After they had gone out into the fields and gathered the grapes and trodden them, they held a festival in the temple of their god. While they were eating and drinking, they cursed Abimelech."

Judges 16:25
"While they were in high spirits, they shouted, 'Bring out Samson to entertain us'. So they called Samson out of the prison, and he performed for them. When they stood him among the pillars..."

1 Samuel 25:36
"When Abigail went to Nabal, he was in the house holding a banquet like that of a king. He was in high spirits and very drunk. So she told him nothing until daybreak."

1 Samuel 30:16
"He led David down, and there they were, scattered over the countryside, eating, drinking and reveling because of the great amount of plunder they had taken from the land of the Philistines and from Judah."

Gal 5:19-21 (KJV)
"Now the works of the flesh are manifest, which are these; Adultery, fornication, un-cleanness, lasciviousness, idolatry, witchcraft, hatred, variance, emulations, wrath, strife, seditions, heresies, envyings, murders, drunkenness, revellings, and such like: of the which I tell you before, as I have also told you in time past, that they which do such things shall not inherit the kingdom of God."

1 Peter 4:3
"For you have spent enough time in the past doing what pagans choose to do - living in debauchery, lust, drunkenness, orgies, carousing and detestable idolatry."

IDLENESS:

Number 12 is idleness. Idleness or laziness is a problem that we see too much of in the body of Christ. People who are just unwilling to work. The Bible states that a man who does not work, should not eat. The body of Christ should adopt and apply that principle. The Scriptures that relate to idleness:

Proverbs 18:9
"One who is slack in his work is brother to one who destroys."

Proverbs 19:15
"Laziness brings on deep sleep, and the shiftless man goes hungry."

Proverbs 22:15
"Folly is bound up in the heart of a child, but the rod of discipline will drive it far from him."

Proverbs 24:30-31
"I went past the field of the sluggard, past the vineyard of the man who lacks judgment; thorns had come up everywhere, the ground was covered with weeds, and the stone wall was in ruins."

Ecclesiastes 10:18
"If a man is lazy, the rafters sag; if his hands are idle, the house leaks."

Matthew 25:26
"His master replied, 'You wicked, lazy servant! So you knew that I harvest where I have not sown and gather where I have not scattered seed?'"

Romans 12:11
"Never be lacking in zeal, but keep your spiritual fervor, serving the Lord."

2 Thessalonians 3:11
"We hear that some among you are idle. They are not busy; they are busybodies."

Hebrews 6:12
"We do not want you to become lazy, but to imitate those who through faith and patience inherit what has been promised."

MALICE:

Number 13 is malice.

Malice means ill will, spite, a desire to hurt others. If one carries malice in the heart toward another or toward themselves, it can pollute a person's entire life. Malice needs to be dealt with by the power of God through the study of God's Word.
Scriptures related to **malice**:

1 Corinthians 5:8
"Therefore, let us keep the Festival, not with the old yeast, the yeast of malice and wickedness, but with bread without yeast, the bread of sincerity and truth."

1 Corinthians 14:20
"Brothers, stop thinking like children. In regard to evil be infants, but in your thinking be adults."

Ephesians 4:31
"Get rid of all bitterness, rage and anger, brawling and slander, along with every form of malice."

Colossians 3:8
"But now you must rid yourselves of all such things as these: anger, rage, malice, slander, and filthy language from your lips."

1 Peter 2:1
"Therefore, rid yourselves of all malice and all deceit, hypocrisy, envy, and slander of every kind."

Examples of **malice**:

Esther 3:6
"Yet having learned who Mordecai's people were, he scorned the idea of killing only Mordecai. Instead Haman looked for a way to destroy all Mordecai's people, the Jews, throughout the whole kingdom of Xerxes."

Psalms 140:3
"They make their tongues as sharp as a serpent's; the poison of vipers is on their lips. Selah"

Proverbs 30:14
"...those whose teeth are swords and whose jaws are set with knives to devour the poor from the earth, the needy from among mankind."

Job 12:20
"He silences the lips of trusted advisers and takes away the discernment of elders."

Isaiah 59:5
"They hatch the eggs of vipers and spin a spider's web. Whoever eats their eggs will die, and when one is broken, an adder is hatched."

Matthew 27:23
"Why? What crime has he committed?" asked Pilate. But they shouted all the louder, 'Crucify him!'"

Acts 7:54
"When they heard this, they were furious and gnashed their teeth at him."

ANXIETY:

Anxiety is an underlying sense of dread or fear of what might happen to an individual. It is a feeling that something bad is likely to happen. The Bible says that God has not given us a spirit of fear, timidity or anxiety, but of love, power, and a sound mind (2 Tim 1:7).

Anxiety can come from the heart when we have past guilt or shame. One must be willing again to look at those things and deal with them from a Biblical viewpoint.

The Scriptures that apply:

Matthew 14:30 (Regarding Peter)
"But when he saw the wind, he was afraid and, beginning to sink, cried out, "Lord, save me!"

Matthew 17:6
"When the disciples heard this, they fell face down to the ground, terrified."

Mark 4:38
"Jesus was in the stern, sleeping on a cushion. The disciples woke him and said to him, "Teacher, don't you care if we drown?"

Mark 5:33
"Then the woman, knowing what had happened to her, came and fell at his feet and, trembling with fear, told him the whole truth."

Mark 16:5
"As they entered the tomb, they saw a young man dressed in a white robe sitting on the right side, and they were alarmed."

Luke 1:12
"When Zechariah saw him, he was startled and was gripped with fear."

Luke 12:11
"When you are brought before synagogues, rulers and authorities, do not worry about how you will defend yourselves or what you will say,..."

Luke 12:25
"Who of you by worrying can add a single hour to his life?"

1 Corinthians 7:32
"I would like you to be free from concern. An unmarried man is concerned about the Lord's affairs-how he can please the Lord."

Philippians 4:6
"Do not be anxious about anything, but in everything, by prayer and petition, with thanksgiving, present your requests to God."

Worldly care is a form of Anxiety:

Psalms 39:6
"Man is a mere phantom as he goes to and fro: He bustles about, but only in vain; he heaps up wealth, not knowing who will get it."

Ecclesiastes 1:13
"I devoted myself to study and to explore by wisdom all that is done under heaven. What a heavy burden God has laid on men!"

Ecclesiastes 2:26
"To the man who pleases him, God gives wisdom, knowledge and happiness, but to the sinner he gives the task of gathering and storing up wealth to hand it over to the one who pleases God. This too is meaningless, a chasing after the wind."

Matthew 6:31
"So do not worry, saying, 'What shall we eat?' or 'What shall we drink?' or 'What shall we wear.'"

Matthew 13:7 & 22
"Other seed fell among thorns, which grew up and choked the plants. The one who received the seed that fell among the thorns is the man who hears the word, but the worries of this life and the deceitfulness of wealth choke it, making it unfruitful."

Luke 10:40
"But Martha was distracted by all the preparations that had to be made. She came to him and asked, "Lord, don't you care that my sister has left me to do the work by myself? Tell her to help me!"

Anxiety is forbidden in these Scriptures:

Psalms 127:2
In vain you rise early and stay up late, toiling for food to eat - for he grants sleep to those he loves.

Matthew 6:25
"Therefore I tell you, do not worry about your life, what you will eat or

drink; or about your body, what you will wear. Is not life more important than food, and the body more important than clothes?"

Luke 10:41
"Martha, Martha," the Lord answered, 'you are worried and upset about many things…"

Luke 12:29
"And do not set your heart on what you will eat or drink; do not worry about it."

Luke 21:34
"Be careful, or your hearts will be weighed down with dissipation, drunkenness and the anxieties of life, and that day will close on you unexpectedly like a trap."

Philippians 4:6
"Do not be anxious about anything, but in everything, by prayer and petition, with thanksgiving, present your requests to God."

1 Peter 5:7
"Cast all your anxiety on him because he cares for you."

It is painful to live under anxiety. It is believed that all psychological troubles come from anxiety. God has given us power over anxiety as we learn to praise Him and deal with the underlying issues within our heart.

PRIDE:

Number 15 is pride.

Pride was the sin of Lucifer. He sought to lift himself up above God. Akin to it would be arrogance, conceit, haughtiness, or boasting.

If pride is in one's heart, it must be dealt with. For, "Pride goes before destruction and a haughty spirit before a fall." Proverbs 16:18

115

The Scriptures include:

Psalms 10:2
"In his arrogance the wicked man hunts down the weak, who are caught in the schemes he devises."

Psalms 73:6
"Therefore pride is their necklace; they clothe themselves with violence."

Psalms 119:21
"You rebuke the arrogant, who are cursed and who stray from your commands."

Proverbs 6:17
"...haughty eyes, a lying tongue, hands that shed innocent blood,..."

Proverbs 11:2
"When pride comes, then comes disgrace, but with humility comes wisdom."

Proverbs 13:10
"Pride only breeds quarrels, but wisdom is found in those who take advice."

Proverbs 16:18
"Pride goes before destruction, a haughty spirit before a fall."

Proverbs 21:4
"Haughty eyes and a proud heart, the lamp of the wicked, are sin!"

Habakkuk 2:4
"See, he is puffed up; his desires are not upright- but the righteous will live by his faith..."

1 John 2:16
"For everything in the world-the cravings of sinful man, the lust of his eyes and the boasting of what he has and does-comes not from the Father but from the world."

Arrogance:

1 Samuel 2:3
"Do not keep talking so proudly or let your mouth speak such arrogance, for the LORD is a God who knows, and by him deeds are weighed."

Psalms 12:4
"We will triumph with our tongues; we own our lips -who is our master?"

Isaiah 13:11
"I will punish the world for its evil, the wicked for their sins. I will put an end to the arrogance of the haughty and will humble the pride of the ruthless."

Hosea 7:10
"Israel's arrogance testifies against him, but despite all this he does not return to the LORD his God or search for him."

Conceit:

Proverbs 3:7
"Do not be wise in your own eyes; fear the LORD and shun evil."

Proverbs 26:5
"Answer a fool according to his folly, or he will be wise in his own eyes."

Proverbs 26:12
"Do you see a man wise in his own eyes? There is more hope for a fool than for him."

Isaiah 5:21
"Woe to those who are wise in their own eyes and clever in their own sight."

Romans 12:6
"We have different gifts, according to the grace given us. If a man's gift is prophesying, let him use it in proportion to his faith."

1 Corinthians 8:2
"The man who thinks he knows something does not yet know as he ought to know."

Galatians 6:3
"If anyone thinks he is something when he is nothing, he deceives himself."

Haughtiness:

2 Samuel 22:28
"You save the humble, but your eyes are on the haughty to bring them low."

Isaiah 3:16
"The LORD says, 'The women of Zion are haughty, walking along with outstretched necks, flirting with their eyes, tripping along with mincing steps, with ornaments jingling on their ankles.'"

Isaiah 16:6
"We have heard of Moab's pride- her overwhelming pride and conceit, her pride and her insolence- but her boasts are empty."

Isaiah 24:4
"The earth dries up and withers, the world languishes and withers, the exalted of the earth languish."

Zephaniah 3:11
"On that day you will not be put to shame for all the wrongs you have done to me, because I will remove from this city those who rejoice in their pride. Never again will you be haughty on my holy hill."

Boasters:

1 Samuel 17:44
"Come here," he said, "and I'll give your flesh to the birds of the air and the beasts of the field!"

1 Kings 20:10
"Then Ben-Hadad sent another message to Ahab: "May the gods deal with me, be it ever so severely, if enough dust remains in Samaria to give each of my men a handful."

Daniel 3:5
"As soon as you hear the sound of the horn, flute, zither, lyre, harp, pipes and all kinds of music, you must fall down and worship the image of gold that King Nebuchadnezzar has set up."

Acts 8:9
"Now for some time a man named Simon had practiced sorcery in the city and amazed all the people of Samaria. He boasted that he was someone great..."

Romans 1:30
"...slanderers, God-haters, insolent, arrogant and boastful; they invent ways of doing evil; they disobey their parents..."

2 Peter 2:18
"For they mouth empty, boastful words and, by appealing to the lustful desires of sinful human nature, they entice people who are just escaping from those who live in error."

CRITICISM:

Next is fault finding or criticism. To criticize is to compare someone falsely and to put others down.

Criticism runs rampant in the church. Many believers constantly try to lift themselves up by putting someone else down. It's usually a sign of great insecurity in a person's life.

The Scriptures that relate to Criticism:

Matthew 9:11
"When the Pharisees saw this, they asked his disciples, "Why does your teacher eat with tax collectors and sinners?"

Matthew 15:2
"Why do your disciples break the tradition of the elders? They don't wash their hands before they eat!"

Mark 2:7
"Why does this fellow talk like that? He's blaspheming! Who can forgive sins but God alone?"

Mark 2:16
"When the teachers of the law who were Pharisees saw him eating with the 'sinners' and tax collectors, they asked his disciples: "Why does he eat with tax collectors and sinners?"

Mark 7:2
"...(and) saw some of his disciples eating food with hands that were 'unclean,' that is, unwashed."

Luke 19:7
"All the people saw this and began to mutter, "He has gone to be the guest of a 'sinner'."

John 6:41
"At this the Jews began to grumble about him because he said, "I am the bread that came down from heaven."

DISOBEDIENCE:

Number 17 is disobedience.

Disobedience is the opposite of obedience, to do the opposite of what God wants. The Biblical references are:

Deuteronomy 11:28
"...the curse if you disobey the commands of the LORD your God and turn from the way that I command you today by following other gods, which you have not known."

1 Samuel 12:15
"But if you do not obey the LORD, and if you rebel against his commands,

his hand will be against you, as it was against your fathers."

1 Samuel 28:18
"Because you did not obey the LORD or carry out his fierce wrath against the Amalekites, the LORD has done this to you today."

1 Kings 13:21
"He cried out to the man of God who had come from Judah, "This is what the LORD says: 'You have defied the word of the LORD and have not kept the command the LORD your God gave you.' "

Jeremiah 12:17
"But if any nation does not listen, I will completely uproot and destroy it," declares the LORD.

Ephesians 5:6
"Let no one deceive you with empty words, for because of such things God's wrath comes on those who are disobedient."

2 Thessalonians 1:8
"He will punish those who do not know God and do not obey the gospel of our Lord Jesus."

1 Timothy 1:9
"We also know that law is made not for the righteous but for lawbreakers and rebels, the ungodly and sinful, the unholy and irreligious; for those who kill their fathers or mothers, for murderers..."

Hebrews 2:2
"For if the message spoken by angels was binding, and every violation and disobedience received its just punishment,..."

Hebrews 2:3
"How shall we escape if we ignore such a great salvation? This salvation, which was first announced by the Lord, was confirmed to us by those who heard him."

Examples of **disobedience**:

Genesis 3:11
"And he said, "Who told you that you were naked? Have you eaten from the tree that I commanded you not to eat from?"

Leviticus 10:1
"Aaron's sons Nadab and Abihu took their censers, put fire in them and added incense; and they offered unauthorized fire before the LORD, contrary to his command."

Numbers 20:11
"Then Moses raised his arm and struck the rock twice with his staff. Water gushed out, and the community and their livestock drank."

Joshua 7:1
"But the Israelites acted unfaithfully in regard to the devoted things; Achan son of Carmi, the son of Zimri, the son of Zerah, of the tribe of Judah, took some of them. So the Lord's anger burned against Israel."

1 Samuel 13:13
"You acted foolishly," Samuel said. "You have not kept the command the LORD your God gave you; if you had, he would have established your kingdom over Israel for all time."

Zephaniah 3:2
"She obeys no one, she accepts no correction. She does not trust in the LORD, she does not draw near to her God."

Jonah 1:1-3
"The word of the LORD came to Jonah son of Amittai: "Go to the great city of Nineveh and preach against it, because its wickedness has come up before me." But Jonah ran away from the LORD and headed for Tarshish. He went down to Joppa, where he found a ship bound for that port. After paying the fare, he went aboard and sailed for Tarshish to flee from the LORD."

REBELLION:

Number 18 rebellion.

The Bible says that rebellion is as the sin of witchcraft. Witchcraft in its fullest form is going completely against God's plan and purpose.

Rebellion is not just having a different opinion in some areas, we can all have different opinions and not be in rebellion. But when we go against the very laws of God to please ourselves, that is rebellion!

The Scriptures:

Deuteronomy 9:23
"And when the LORD sent you out from Kadesh Barnea, he said, "Go up and take possession of the land I have given you." But you rebelled against the command of the LORD your God. You did not trust him or obey him."

Deuteronomy 9:24
"You have been rebellious against the LORD ever since I have known you."

1 Samuel 15:23
"For rebellion is like the sin of divination, and arrogance like the evil of idolatry. Because you have rejected the word of the LORD, he has rejected you as king."

Nehemiah 9:17
"They refused to listen and failed to remember the miracles you performed among them. They became stiff-necked and in their rebellion appointed a leader in order to return to their slavery. But you are a forgiving God, gracious and compassionate, slow to anger and abounding in love. Therefore you did not desert them."

Psalms 68:6
"God sets the lonely in families, he leads forth the prisoners with singing;

but the rebellious live in a sun-scorched land."

Isaiah 65:2-5
"All day long I have held out my hands to an obstinate people, who walk in ways not good, pursuing their own imaginations - a people who continually provoke me to my very face, offering sacrifices in gardens and burning incense on altars of brick; who sit among the graves and spend their nights keeping secret vigil; who eat the flesh of pigs, and whose pots hold broth of unclean meat; who say, 'Keep away; don't come near me, for I am too sacred for you!' Such people are smoke in my nostrils, a fire that keeps burning all day."

Jeremiah 5:5
"So I will go to the leaders and speak to them; surely they know the way of the LORD, the requirements of their God. But with one accord they too had broken off the yoke and torn off the bonds."

Ezekiel 2:3
"He said: "Son of man, I am sending you to the Israelites, to a rebellious nation that has rebelled against me; they and their fathers have been in revolt against me to this very day."

Ezekiel 2:4
"The people to whom I am sending you are obstinate and stubborn. Say to them, 'This is what the Sovereign LORD says.'"

Ezekiel 12:2
"Son of man, you are living among a rebellious people. They have eyes to see but do not see and ears to hear but do not hear, for they are a rebellious people."

LYING:

Number 19 lying.

The Bible says that Satan is a liar and the father of all lies. A lie could include not telling the whole truth and also telling a blatant lie.

Frankly, there is no difference between a white lie or black lie. A lie is a lie. God wants us to speak the truth. He wants us to speak the truth, but always speak it in love.

There are many Scriptures that speak about lying.

Genesis 12:11-13
"As he was about to enter Egypt, he said to his wife Sarai, "I know what a beautiful woman you are. When they see you, they will say, 'This is his wife.' Then they will kill me but will let you live. Say you are my sister, so that I will be treated well for your sake and my life will be spared because of you."

Genesis 12:19
"Why did you say, 'She is my sister,' so that I took her to be my wife? Now then, here is your wife. Take her and go!"

Genesis 27:18-30
"He went to his father and said, "My father." "Yes, my son," he answered. "Who is it?" Jacob said to his father, "I am Esau your firstborn. I have done as you told me. Please sit up and eat some of my game so that you may give me your blessing." Isaac asked his son, "How did you find it so quickly, my son?" "The LORD your God gave me success," he replied. Then Isaac said to Jacob, "Come near so I can touch you, my son, to know whether you really are my son Esau or not." Jacob went close to his father Isaac, who touched him and said, "The voice is the voice of Jacob, but the hands are the hands of Esau." He did not recognize him for his hands were hairy like those of his brother Esau; so he blessed him. "Are you really my son Esau?" he asked. "I am," he replied. Then he said, "My son, bring me some of your game to eat, so that I may give you my blessing." Jacob brought it to him and he ate; and he brought some wine and he drank. Then his father Isaac said to him, "Come here, my son, and kiss me." So he went to him and kissed him. When Isaac caught the smell of his clothes, he blessed him and said, "Ah, the smell of my son is like the smell of a field that the LORD has blessed. May God give you of heaven's dew and of earth's richness - an abundance of grain and new wine." May nations serve you and peoples bow down to you. Be lord over your brothers, and may the sons of your mother bow down to you. May those who curse you be cursed and those who bless you be blessed." After

Isaac finished blessing him and Jacob had scarcely left his father's presence, his brother Esau came in from hunting."

1 Kings 13:18
"The old prophet answered, "I too am a prophet, as you are. And an angel said to me by the word of the LORD: 'Bring him back with you to your house so that he may eat bread and drink water.'" (But he was lying to him.)"

2 Kings 6:19
"Elisha told them, "This is not the road and this is not the city. Follow me, and I will lead you to the man you are looking for." And he led them to Samaria."

Examples of lying:

Genesis 3:4
"You will not surely die," the serpent said to the woman."

Judges 3:20-21
"Ehud then approached him while he was sitting alone in the upper room of his summer palace and said, "I have a message from God for you." As the king rose from his seat, Ehud reached with his left hand, drew the sword from his right thigh and plunged it into the king's belly."

2 Samuel 13:6
"So Amnon lay down and pretended to be ill. When the king came to see him, Amnon said to him, "I would like my sister Tamar to come and make some special bread in my sight, so I may eat from her hand."

2 Kings 5:22
"Everything is all right," Gehazi answered. "My master sent me to say, 'Two young men from the company of the prophets have just come to me from the hill country of Ephraim. Please give them a talent of silver and two sets of clothing.'"

Matthew 2:8
"He sent them to Bethlehem and said, "Go and make a careful search for the child. As soon as you find him, report to me, so that I too may go and

worship him."

Another word for lying is **deception:**

Psalms 36:2
"For in his own eyes he flatters himself too much to detect or hate his sin."

Isaiah 44:20
"He feeds on ashes, a deluded heart misleads him; he cannot save himself, or say, "Is not this thing in my right hand a lie?"

Galatians 6:3
"If anyone thinks he is something when he is nothing, he deceives himself."

James 1:22
"Do not merely listen to the word, and so deceive yourselves. Do what it says."

James 1:26
"If anyone considers himself religious and yet does not keep a tight rein on his tongue, he deceives himself and his religion is worthless."

1 John 1:8
"If we claim to be without sin, we deceive ourselves and the truth is not in us."

Revelation 3:17
"You say, 'I am rich; I have acquired wealth and do not need a thing.' But you do not realize that you are wretched, pitiful, poor, blind and naked."

The Bible says we're not to be **deceived**:

Matthew 24:4
"Jesus answered: "Watch out that no one deceives you."

1 Corinthians 6:9
"Do you not know that the wicked will not inherit the kingdom of God? Do not be deceived: Neither the sexually immoral, nor idolaters, nor

adulterers, nor male prostitutes, nor homosexual offenders."

1 Corinthians 15:33
"Do not be misled: "Bad company corrupts good character."

Galatians 6:7
"Do not be deceived: God cannot be mocked. A man reaps what he sows."

Ephesians 5:6
"Let no one deceive you with empty words, for because of such things God's wrath comes on those who are disobedient."

2 Thessalonians 2:3
"Don't let anyone deceive you in any way, for that day will not come until the rebellion occurs and the man of lawlessness is revealed, the man doomed to destruction."

1 John 3:7
"Dear children, do not let anyone lead you astray. He who does what is right is righteous, just as He is righteous."

Fraud is another word for deception or lying:

Leviticus 19:13
"Do not defraud your neighbor or rob him. Do not hold back the wages of a hired man overnight."

Mark 10:19
"You know the commandments: 'Do not murder, do not commit adultery, do not steal, do not give false testimony, do not defraud, honor your father and mother.'"

1 Corinthians 6:8
"Instead, you yourselves cheat and do wrong, and you do this to your brothers."

WRATH:

The final negative word is wrath:

Wrath is anger… out of control! The Bible speaks so very strongly against it.

The references include:

Genesis 4:5
"But on Cain and his offering he did not look with favor. So Cain was very angry, and his face was downcast."

1 Samuel 18:8
"Saul was very angry; this refrain galled him. "They have credited David with tens of thousands," he thought, "but me with only thousands. What more can he get but the kingdom?"

2 Chronicles 16:10
"Asa was angry with the seer because of this; he was so enraged that he put him in prison. At the same time Asa brutally oppressed some of the people."

Esther 3:5
"When Haman saw that Mordecai would not kneel down or pay him honor, he was enraged."

Amos 1:11
"This is what the LORD says: "For three sins of Edom, even for four, I will not turn back my wrath. Because he pursued his brother with a sword, stifling all compassion, because his anger raged continually and his fury flamed unchecked,…"

Psalms 37:8
"Refrain from anger and turn from wrath; do not fret - it leads only to evil."

Proverbs 16:32
"Better a patient man than a warrior, a man who controls his temper than one who takes a city."

Proverbs 19:11
"A man's wisdom gives him patience; it is to his glory to overlook an

offense."

Proverbs 22:24
"Do not make friends with a hot-tempered man, do not associate with one easily angered."

Proverbs 27:4
"Anger is cruel and fury overwhelming, but who can stand before jealousy?"

Ecclesiastes 7:9
"Do not be quickly provoked in your spirit, for anger resides in the lap of fools."

Matthew 5:22
"But I tell you that anyone who is angry with his brother will be subject to judgment. Again, anyone who says to his brother, 'Raca,' is answerable to the Sanhedrin. But anyone who says, 'You fool!' will be in danger of the fire of hell."

Luke 4:28
"All the people in the synagogue were furious when they heard this."

Luke 6:11
"But they were furious and began to discuss with one another what they might do to Jesus."

Acts 19:28
"When they heard this, they were furious and began shouting: "Great is Artemis of the Ephesians!"

James 1:19-20
"My dear brothers, take note of this: Everyone should be quick to listen, slow to speak and slow to become angry, for man's anger does not bring about the righteous life that God desires."

If you try to go through all these things at once you may end up in a place of great depression. This is why I recommend that you combine putting off the old, and putting on the new.

Don't just do the negatives first, rather, go about putting on the 20 new characteristics of the heart.

CHAPTER ELEVEN

The Positive 20

Many of these positive traits are taken from Galatians 5 which presents the fruit of the Spirit. With the fruit of the Spirit, and complementary to it, are other characteristics of significance to your growth and change.

The 20 positives:

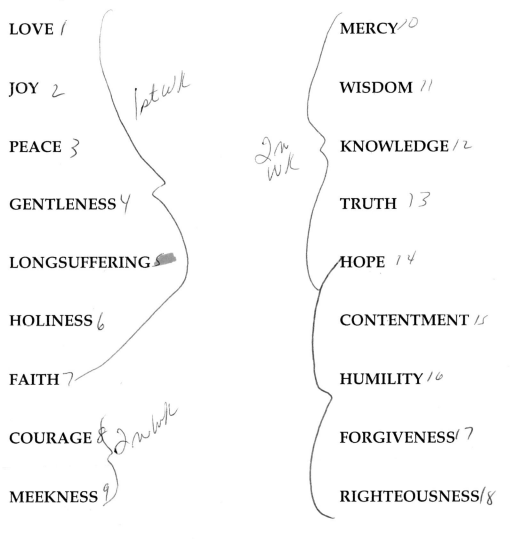

LOVE *1*

JOY *2*

PEACE *3*

GENTLENESS *4*

LONGSUFFERING *5*

HOLINESS *6*

FAITH *7*

COURAGE *8*

MEEKNESS *9*

MERCY *10*

WISDOM *11*

KNOWLEDGE *12*

TRUTH *13*

HOPE *14*

CONTENTMENT *15*

HUMILITY *16*

FORGIVENESS *17*

RIGHTEOUSNESS *18*

1st wk

2nd wk

2nd wk

LOVE:

The first word in this illustrious list is Love. This is a word that is often misused or used in different ways.

For a very wonderful study on Love, I suggest Dr. Ken Chant's book entitled, "Christian Life: Patterns of Gracious Living."

There are three primary types of love that we find in the Greek.

First: **eros** or erotic love, having to do with romantic and/or sexual love.

Second: **phileo** which is brotherly love or brotherly kindness especially within a family.

Third: **agape** which means God's love. It is not natural for us to have a kind of love that is self sacrificing for the sake of others, yet that is the love that God has and wants us to 'put on'. This is not a garment that we wear just on the outside but what is within.

Some Scriptures that express brotherly love include:

Proverbs 10:12
"Hatred stirs up dissension, but love covers over all wrongs."

1 Corinthians 13:1-12
"If I speak in the tongues of men and of angels, but have not love, I am only a resounding gong or a clanging cymbal. If I have the gift of prophecy and can fathom all mysteries and all knowledge, and if I have a faith that can move mountains, but have not love, I am nothing. If I give all I possess to the poor and surrender my body to the flames, but have not love, I gain nothing. Love is patient, love is kind. It does not envy, it does not boast, it is not proud. It is not rude, it is not self-seeking, it is not easily angered, it keeps no record of wrongs. Love does not delight in evil but rejoices with the truth. It always protects, always trusts, always hopes, always perseveres. Love never fails. But where there are prophecies,

they will cease; where there are tongues, they will be stilled; where there is knowledge, it will pass away. For we know in part and we prophesy in part, but when perfection comes, the imperfect disappears. When I was a child, I talked like a child, I thought like a child, I reasoned like a child. When I became a man, I put childish ways behind me. Now we see but a poor reflection as in a mirror; then we shall see face to face. Now I know in part; then I shall know fully, even as I am fully known."

Galatians 5:13
"You, my brothers, were called to be free. But do not use your freedom to indulge the sinful nature; rather, serve one another in love."

"And this is my prayer: that your love may abound more and more in knowledge and depth of insight…"

1 Thessalonians 4:9
"Now about brotherly love we do not need to write to you, for you yourselves have been taught by God to love each other."

1 Peter 4:8
"Above all, love each other deeply, because love covers over a multitude of sins."

1 John 2:10
"Whoever loves his brother lives in the light, and there is nothing in him to make him stumble."

1 John 4:21
"And he has given us this command: Whoever loves God must also love his brother."

Love expressed:

Genesis 29:20
"So Jacob served seven years to get Rachel, but they seemed like only a few days to him because of his love for her."

Esther 2:17
"Now the king was attracted to Esther more than to any of the other

women, and she won his favor and approval more than any of the other virgins. So he set a royal crown on her head and made her queen instead of Vashti."

Proverbs 5:19
"A loving doe, a graceful deer - may her breasts satisfy you always, may you ever be captivated by her love."

Song of Songs 8:7
"Many waters cannot quench love; rivers cannot wash it away. If one were to give all the wealth of his house for love, it would be utterly scorned."

Ephesians 5:28
"In this same way, husbands ought to love their wives as their own bodies. He who loves his wife loves himself."

Ephesians 5:33
"However, each one of you also must love his wife as he loves himself, and the wife must respect her husband."

Colossians 3:19
"Husbands, love your wives and do not be harsh with them."

In his letter to the Corinthians Paul wrote: Three things abide, **FAITH, HOPE** and **LOVE.** He also said the greatest of these is **LOVE!**

If we live in a loving relationship, right with God and right with one another, we fulfill the whole law.

JOY:

As a child I was taught that joy was spelled:

Jesus first;
Others next;
Yourself last!

There is a measure of truth in that simple equation. Joy is the exhilaration or contentment that goes beyond normal happiness. Happiness has to do with circumstances. Joy is an abiding presence.

Joy is exemplified in the following Scriptures:

Luke 2:10
"But the angel said to them, "Do not be afraid. I bring you good news of great joy that will be for all the people."

Luke 15:5
"And when he finds (the lamb), he joyfully puts it on his shoulders and goes home."

John 17:13
"I am coming to you now, but I say these things while I am still in the world, so that they may have the full measure of my joy within them."

Hebrews 12:2
"Let us fix our eyes on Jesus, the author and perfecter of our faith, who for the joy set before him endured the cross, scorning its shame, and sat down at the right hand of the throne of God."

Great **Joy**:

Ezra 3:12
"But many of the older priests and Levites and family heads, who had seen the former temple, wept aloud when they saw the foundation of this temple being laid, while many others shouted for joy."

Job 38:7
"While the morning stars sang together and all the angels shouted for joy?"

Matthew 2:10 (The Wisemen)
"When they saw the star, they were overjoyed."

Matthew 28:8 (At the tomb)
"So the women hurried away from the tomb, afraid yet filled with joy, and ran to tell his disciples."

Luke 24:52
"Then they worshiped him and returned to Jerusalem with great joy."

Acts 15:3
"The church sent them on their way, and as they traveled through Phoenicia and Samaria, they told how the Gentiles had been converted. This news made all the brothers very glad."

Joy promised:

Nehemiah 8:10
"Nehemiah said, "Go and enjoy choice food and sweet drinks, and send some to those who have nothing prepared. This day is sacred to our Lord. Do not grieve, for the joy of the LORD is your strength."

Psalms 30:5
"For his anger lasts only a moment, but his favor lasts a lifetime; weeping may remain for a night, but rejoicing comes in the morning."

Psalms 89:16
"They rejoice in your name all day long; they exult in your righteousness."

Psalms 126:5
"Those who sow in tears will reap with songs of joy."

Psalms 132:16
"I will clothe her priests with salvation, and her saints will ever sing for joy."

Isaiah 12:3
"With joy you will draw water from the wells of salvation."

Isaiah 35:10
"...and the ransomed of the LORD will return. They will enter Zion with

singing; everlasting joy will crown their heads. Gladness and joy will overtake them, and sorrow and sighing will flee away."

Luke 2:10
"But the angel said to them, "Do not be afraid. I bring you good news of great joy that will be for all the people."

John 15:11
"I have told you this so that my joy may be in you and that your joy may be complete."

John 16:24
"Until now you have not asked for anything in my name. Ask and you will receive, and your joy will be complete."

John 17:13
"I am coming to you now, but I say these things while I am still in the world, so that they may have the full measure of my joy within them."

Romans 14:17
"For the kingdom of God is not a matter of eating and drinking, but of righteousness, peace and joy in the Holy Spirit,..."

Joy restored:

Psalms 30:11
"You turned my wailing into dancing; you removed my sackcloth and clothed me with joy."

Isaiah 61:3
"...and provide for those who grieve in Zion - to bestow on them a crown of beauty instead of ashes, the oil of gladness instead of mourning, and a garment of praise instead of a spirit of despair. They will be called oaks of righteousness, a planting of the LORD for the display of his splendor."

Jeremiah 30:19
"From them will come songs of thanksgiving and the sound of rejoicing. I will add to their numbers, and they will not be decreased; I will bring them honor, and they will not be disdained."

Jeremiah 31:13

"Then maidens will dance and be glad, young men and old as well. I will turn their mourning into gladness; I will give them comfort and joy instead of sorrow."

Hosea 2:15

"Then I will give her vineyards from there, and the valley of anchor as a door of hope. And she will sing there as in the days of her youth, as in the day when she came up from the land of Egypt."

Special reasons for **Joy**:

Ezra 6:22

"For seven days they celebrated with joy the Feast of Unleavened Bread, because the LORD had filled them with joy by changing the attitude of the king of Assyria, so that he assisted them in the work on the house of God, the God of Israel."

Psalms 126:2

"Our mouths were filled with laughter, our tongues with songs of joy. Then it was said among the nations, "The LORD has done great things for them."

Isaiah 61:10

"I delight greatly in the LORD; my soul rejoices in my God. For he has clothed me with garments of salvation and arrayed me in a robe of righteousness, as a bridegroom adorns his head like a priest, and as a bride adorns herself with her jewels."

Acts 8:39

"When they came up out of the water, the Spirit of the Lord suddenly took Philip away, and the eunuch did not see him again, but went on his way rejoicing."

Romans 5:11

"Not only is this so, but we also rejoice in God through our Lord Jesus Christ, through whom we have now received reconciliation."

2 Corinthians 7:4
"I have great confidence in you; I take great pride in you. I am greatly encouraged; in all our troubles my joy knows no bounds."

1 Peter 1:8
"Though you have not seen him, you love him; and even though you do not see him now, you believe in him and are filled with an inexpressible and glorious joy."

Joy is found all throughout the Word of God.

Joy includes gladness and rejoicing:

Gladness: instances of joy that are expressed because of deliverances from fiery trials

Rejoicing: an activity which comes from having joy and is something that is to be characteristic of the individual Christian. When people feel joy often times they shout and laugh and enjoy the various aspects of living life abundantly.

PEACE:

Peace is a sense of tranquility, a place of rest which has been promised to every believer.

Scriptures that speak of peace:

Psalms 4:8
"I will lie down and sleep in peace, for you alone, O LORD, make me dwell in safety."

Psalms 29:11
"The LORD gives strength to his people; the LORD blesses his people with peace."

Psalms 119:165
"Great peace have they who love your law, and nothing can make them

stumble."

Proverbs 3:17
"Her ways are pleasant ways, and all her paths are peace."

Isaiah 26:3
"You will keep in perfect peace him whose mind is steadfast, because he trusts in you."

Isaiah 48:18
"If only you had paid attention to my commands, your peace would have been like a river, your righteousness like the waves of the sea."

Luke 1:78-79
"...because of the tender mercy of our God, by which the rising sun will come to us from heaven to shine on those living in darkness and in the shadow of death, to guide our feet into the path of peace."

John 14:27
"Peace I leave with you; my peace I give you. I do not give to you as the world gives. Do not let your hearts be troubled and do not be afraid."

John 16:33
"I have told you these things, so that in me you may have peace. In this world you will have trouble. But take heart! I have overcome the world."

Acts 10:36
"You know the message God sent to the people of Israel, telling the good news of peace through Jesus Christ, who is Lord of all."

Romans 5:1
"Therefore, since we have been justified through faith, we have peace with God through our Lord Jesus Christ."

Romans 8:6
"The mind of sinful man is death, but the mind controlled by the Spirit is life and peace."

Romans 14:17
"For the kingdom of God is not a matter of eating and drinking, but of righteousness, peace and joy in the Holy Spirit."

Galatians 5:22-23
"But the fruit of the Spirit is love, joy, peace, patience, kindness, goodness, faithfulness, gentleness and self-control. Against such things there is no law."

Ephesians 2:14
"For he himself is our peace, who has made the two one and has destroyed the barrier, the dividing wall of hostility."

Colossians 1:20
"...and through him to reconcile to himself all things, whether things on earth or things in heaven, by making peace through his blood, shed on the cross."

Peace is something that must be sought:

Joshua 22:21-23 (KJV)
"Then the children of Reuben and the children of Gad and the half tribe of Manasseh answered, and said unto the heads of the thousands of Israel, "The LORD God of gods, the LORD God of gods, he knoweth, and Israel he shall know; if it be in rebellion, or if in transgression against the LORD, (save us not this day,). That we have built us an altar to turn from following the LORD, or if to offer thereon burnt offering or meat offering, or if to offer peace offerings thereon, let the LORD himself require it;..."

Psalms 34:14
"Turn from evil and do good; seek peace and pursue it."

Isaiah 27:5
"Or else let them come to me for refuge; let them make peace with me, yes, let them make peace with me."

Colossians 3:15
"Let the peace of Christ rule in your hearts, since as members of one body

you were called to peace. And be thankful."

Another word for peace is rest or Sabbath.

In Hebrews 4, the author says that we must labor that we might enter into our rest. So there is a rest provided for the people of God. The desire for peace or rest is the reason for the journey across the wilderness.

The promise to go into the Promised Land, was the promise to enter into the rest or a place of peace in God. This wonderful place of peace often comes when we walk through the "valley of the shadow of death" as David did.

When we come to the other side of the valley we truly fear no evil. It is then that we know **Peace** in the presence of the Lord.

GENTLENESS:

One of the outstanding characteristics of Jesus' ministry, especially to women and children, was that of great kindness and gentleness.

Jesus had unlimited power and authority yet He dealt with the weak and hurting with unbelievable kindness and gentleness.

This should be a characteristic of every Christian, especially those in leadership!

Scriptures include:

Romans 12:10
"Be devoted to one another in brotherly love. Honor one another above yourselves."

1 Corinthians 13:4
"Love is patient, love is kind. It does not envy, it does not boast, it is not proud."

Ephesians 4:32
"Be kind and compassionate to one another, forgiving each other, just as in Christ God forgave you."

Colossians 3:12
"Therefore, as God's chosen people, holy and dearly loved, clothe yourselves with compassion, kindness, humility, gentleness and patience."

2 Peter 1:5-7
"For this very reason, make every effort to add to your faith goodness; and to goodness, knowledge; and to knowledge, self-control; and to self-control, perseverance; and to perseverance, godliness; and to godliness, brotherly kindness; and to brotherly kindness, love."

LONGSUFFERING:

Longsuffering or patience or endurance is an ability given by God. It is part of the fruit of the Spirit.

To endure difficult times graciously we certainly need God's grace. Thankfully it has been given to us by the Holy Spirit.

Patience and **longsuffering**:

2 Thessalonians 1:4
"Therefore, among God's churches we boast about your perseverance and faith in all the persecutions and trials you are enduring."

Hebrews 6:15
"And so after waiting patiently, Abraham received what was promised."

James 5:11
"As you know, we consider blessed those who have persevered. You have heard of Job's perseverance and have seen what the Lord finally brought about. The Lord is full of compassion and mercy."

Revelation 1:9-20
"I, John, your brother and companion in the suffering and kingdom and patient endurance that are ours in Jesus, was on the island of Patmos

because of the word of God and the testimony of Jesus. On the Lord's Day I was in the Spirit, and I heard behind me a loud voice like a trumpet, which said: "Write on a scroll what you see and send it to the seven churches: to Ephesus, Smyrna, Pergamum, Thyatira, Sardis, Philadelphia and Laodicea. I turned around to see the voice that was speaking to me. And when I turned I saw seven golden lampstands, and among the lampstands was someone 'like a son of man,' dressed in a robe reaching down to his feet and with a golden sash around his chest. His head and hair were white like wool, as white as snow, and his eyes were like blazing fire. His feet were like bronze glowing in a furnace, and his voice was like the sound of rushing waters. In his right hand he held seven stars, and out of his mouth came a sharp double-edged sword. His face was like the sun shining in all its brilliance. When I saw him, I fell at his feet as though dead. Then he placed his right hand on me and said: "Do not be afraid. I am the First and the Last. I am the Living One; I was dead, and behold I am alive for ever and ever! And I hold the keys of death and Hades. Write, therefore, what you have seen, what is now and what will take place later. The mystery of the seven stars that you saw in my right hand and of the seven golden lampstands is this: The seven stars are the angels of the seven churches, and the seven lampstands are the seven churches."

Revelation 2:1-2
"To the angel of the church in Ephesus write: "These are the words of him who holds the seven stars in his right hand and walks among the seven golden lampstands: I know your deeds, your hard work and your perseverance. I know that you cannot tolerate wicked men, that you have tested those who claim to be apostles but are not, and have found them false."

Revelation 14:12
"This calls for patient endurance on the part of the saints who obey God's commandments and remain faithful to Jesus."

Longsuffering and **patience** in waiting for God:

Psalms 37:7
"Be still before the LORD and wait patiently for him; do not fret when men succeed in their ways, when they carry out their wicked schemes."

146

Psalms 41:1-13

"Blessed is he who has regard for the weak; the LORD delivers him in times of trouble. The LORD will protect him and preserve his life; he will bless him in the land and not surrender him to the desire of his foes. The LORD will sustain him on his sickbed and restore him from his bed of illness. I said, "O LORD, have mercy on me; heal me, for I have sinned against you." My enemies say of me in malice, "When will he die and his name perish?" Whenever one comes to see me, he speaks falsely, while his heart gathers slander; then he goes out and spreads it abroad. All my enemies whisper together against me; they imagine the worst for me, saying, "A vile disease has beset him; he will never get up from the place where he lies." Even my close friend, whom I trusted, he who shared my bread, has lifted up his heel against me. But you, O LORD, have mercy on me; raise me up, that I may repay them. I know that you are pleased with me, for my enemy does not triumph over me. In my integrity you uphold me and set me in your presence forever. Praise be to the LORD, the God of Israel, from everlasting to everlasting. Amen and Amen."

Isaiah 25:9

"In that day they will say, "Surely this is our God; we trusted in him, and he saved us. This is the LORD, we trusted in him; let us rejoice and be glad in his salvation."

Isaiah 26:8

"Yes, LORD, walking in the way of your laws, we wait for you; your name and renown are the desire of our hearts."

Isaiah 33:2

"O LORD, be gracious to us; we long for you. Be our strength every morning, our salvation in time of distress."

Acts 1:4

"On one occasion, while he was eating with them, he gave them this command: "Do not leave Jerusalem, but wait for the gift my Father promised, which you have heard me speak about."

Other Scriptures relating to **longsuffering**:

Ecclesiastes 7:8
"The end of a matter is better than its beginning, and patience is better than pride."

Luke 21:19
"By standing firm you will gain life."

Romans 12:12
"Be joyful in hope, patient in affliction, faithful in prayer."

Titus 2:2
"Teach the older men to be temperate, worthy of respect, self-controlled, and sound in faith, in love and in endurance."

Hebrews 10:36
"You need to persevere so that when you have done the will of God, you will receive what he has promised."

James 1:4
"Perseverance must finish its work so that you may be mature and complete, not lacking anything."

James 5:7
"Be patient, then, brothers, until the Lord's coming. See how the farmer waits for the land to yield its valuable crop and how patient he is for the autumn and spring rains."

HOLINESS:

One of the primary characteristics of God is holiness. God is holy. He is perfect. He is completely set aside, sanctified.

God says we are to be holy as He is holy. Holiness is not something we can do on our own. It is not something we attain by doing right or looking good. It is an inner-characteristic made available to us through Jesus Christ.

Scriptures in which we see **holiness** spoken of and dealt with:

Genesis 17:1
"When Abram was ninety-nine years old, the LORD appeared to him and said, "I am God Almighty; walk before me and be blameless."

Matthew 5:48
"Be perfect, therefore, as your heavenly Father is perfect."

2 Corinthians 13:11
"Finally, brothers, good-by. Aim for perfection, listen to my appeal, be of one mind, live in peace. And the God of love and peace will be with you."

Ephesians 4:13
"...until we all reach unity in the faith and in the knowledge of the Son of God and become mature, attaining to the whole measure of the fullness of Christ."

Philippians 3:15
"All of us who are mature should take such a view of things. And if on some point you think differently, that too God will make clear to you."

Colossians 1:28
"We proclaim him, admonishing and teaching everyone with all wisdom, so that we may present everyone perfect in Christ."

2 Timothy 3:17
"...so that the man of God may be thoroughly equipped for every good work."

James 1:4
"Perseverance must finish its work so that you may be mature and complete, not lacking anything."

1 Peter 5:10
"And the God of all grace, who called you to his eternal glory in Christ, after you have suffered a little while, will himself restore you and make you strong, firm and steadfast."

Holiness is Christ's perfection:

Hebrews 2:10
"In bringing many sons to glory, it was fitting that God, for whom and through whom everything exists, should make the author of their salvation perfect through suffering."

Hebrews 5:9
"...and, once made perfect, he became the source of eternal salvation for all who obey him"

Hebrews 7:28
"For the law appoints as high priests men who are weak; but the oath, which came after the law, appointed the Son, who has been made perfect forever."

FAITH:

"Faith is often talked about in the body of Christ. The Bible says without faith it is impossible to please God (Hebrews 11:6). Faith is one of the major characteristics that we must be "put on."

It is part of the fruit of the Spirit.

The Bible says: *"Faith is the substance of things hoped for, the evidence of things not seen"* (Hebrews 11:1).

It helps to create spiritual substance. Romans 12:3 says God has dealt to every man the measure of faith. We have enough faith to live life fully and completely as God intends.

There is much to be learned about faith. For more information on faith, I would refer you to Dr. Ken Chant's book, *Faith Dynamics*.

Scriptures on **Faith**:

2 Chronicles 20:20
"Early in the morning they left for the Desert of Tekoa. As they set out,

Jehoshaphat stood and said, "Listen to me, Judah and people of Jerusalem! Have faith in the LORD your God and you will be upheld; have faith in his prophets and you will be successful."

Matthew 9:29-30
"Then he touched their eyes and said, "According to your faith will it be done to you"; and their sight was restored. Jesus warned them sternly, "See that no one knows about this."

Matthew 17:20
"He replied, "Because you have so little faith. I tell you the truth, if you have faith as small as a mustard seed, you can say to this mountain, 'Move from here to there' and it will move. Nothing will be impossible for you."

Mark 9:23
"'If you can'?" Jesus asked. "Anything is possible if you have faith."

Luke 17:5
"The apostles said to the Lord, "Increase our faith!"

Romans 10:17
"Consequently, faith comes from hearing the message, and the message is heard through the word of Christ."

Romans 14:23
"But the man who has doubts is condemned if he eats, because his eating is not from faith; and everything that does not come from faith is sin."

Galatians 5:6
"For in Christ Jesus neither circumcision nor uncircumcision has any value. The only thing that counts is faith expressing itself through love."

Hebrews 11:1
"Now faith is being sure of what we hope for and certain of what we do not see."

James 2:17
"In the same way, faith by itself, if it is not accompanied by action, is

dead."

James 1:5-6
"If any of you lacks wisdom, he should ask God, who gives generously to all without finding fault, and it will be given to him. But when he asks, he must believe and not doubt, because he who doubts is like a wave of the sea, blown and tossed by the wind."

1 John 3:23
"And this is his command: to believe in the name of his Son, Jesus Christ, and to love one another as he commanded us."

1 John 5:4
"...for everyone born of God overcomes the world. This is the victory that has overcome the world, even our faith."

These references will get you started but I encourage you to look up as many Scriptures as you can on faith. Especially the men and women in the Bible. The Old Testament reveals how many of them lived. You will find many listed in the "Faith Hall of Fame" in Hebrews 11.

COURAGE:

The next characteristic is courage. Courage is a type of fearlessness in God. The ability to take action even if it's against one's own personal survival and best interest.

Courage is the willingness to stand for what is right and true.

The church needs men and women of courage! It is a characteristic your heart needs to put on.

Scriptures that speak of **courage:**

Numbers 13:20
"How is the soil? Is it fertile or poor? Are there trees on it or not? Do your best to bring back some of the fruit of the land." (It was the season for the first ripe grapes.)

Deuteronomy 31:6
"Be strong and courageous. Do not be afraid or terrified because of them, for the LORD your God goes with you; he will never leave you nor forsake you."

2 Chronicles 19:11
"Amariah the chief priest will be over you in any matter concerning the LORD, and Zebadiah son of Ishmael, the leader of the tribe of Judah, will be over you in any matter concerning the king, and the Levites will serve as officials before you. Act with courage, and may the LORD be with those who do well."

2 Chronicles 32:7
"Be strong and courageous. Do not be afraid or discouraged because of the king of Assyria and the vast army with him, for there is a greater power with us than with him."

Ezra 10:4
"Rise up; this matter is in your hands. We will support you, so take courage and do it."

Examples of **courage**:

Joshua 14:12 (Caleb)
"Now give me this hill country that the LORD promised me that day. You yourself heard then that the Anakites were there and their cities were large and fortified, but, the LORD helping me, I will drive them out just as he said."

1 Samuel 14:6
"Jonathan said to his young armor-bearer, "Come, let's go over to the outpost of those uncircumcised fellows. Perhaps the LORD will act in our behalf. Nothing can hinder the LORD from saving, whether by many or by few."

Nehemiah 6:11
"But I said, "Should a man like me run away? Or should one like me go into the temple to save his life? I will not go!"

Daniel 3:16-17
"Shadrach, Meshach and Abednego replied to the king, "O Nebuchadnezzar, we do not need to defend ourselves before you in this matter. If we are thrown into the blazing furnace, the God we serve is able to save us from it, and he will rescue us from your hand, O king."

Daniel 6:10
"Now when Daniel learned that the decree had been published, he went home to his upstairs room where the windows opened toward Jerusalem. Three times a day he got down on his knees and prayed, giving thanks to his God, just as he had done before."

Another characteristic similar to this is **fearlessness**. We see that in:

Psalms 3:6
"I will not fear the tens of thousands drawn up against me on every side."

Psalms 27:3
"Though an army besiege me, my heart will not fear; though war break out against me, even then will I be confident."

Psalms 91:5
"You will not fear the terror of night, nor the arrow that flies by day,…"

Psalms 118:6
"The LORD is with me; I will not be afraid. What can man do to me?"

Proverbs 3:24
"When you lie down, you will not be afraid; when you lie down, your sleep will be sweet."

Isaiah 12:2
"Surely God is my salvation; I will trust and not be afraid. The LORD, the LORD, is my strength and my song; he has become my salvation."

John 5:21
"For just as the Father raises the dead and gives them life, even so the Son gives life to whom he is pleased to give it."

MEEKNESS:

Number 9 is meekness.

Meekness has been described as a quiet strength, that of knowing who you are in Christ. When you know who you are in God and you are in right relationship with Him, you have a quiet strength of character.

Meekness is described in:

Zephaniah 2:3
"Seek the LORD, all you humble of the land, you who do what he commands. Seek righteousness, seek humility; perhaps you will be sheltered on the day of the Lord's anger."

Luke 6:29
"If someone strikes you on one cheek, turn to him the other also. If someone takes your cloak, do not stop him from taking your tunic."

Galatians 5:22-23
"But the fruit of the Spirit is love, joy, peace, patience, kindness, goodness, faithfulness, gentleness (meekness) and self-control. Against such things there is no law."

2 Timothy 2:25
"Those who oppose him he must gently instruct, in the hope that God will grant them repentance leading them to a knowledge of the truth,"

James 1:21
"Therefore, get rid of all moral filth and the evil that is so prevalent and humbly accept the word planted in you, which can save you."

1 Peter 3:4
"Instead, it should be that of your inner self, the unfading beauty of a gentle and quiet spirit, which is of great worth in God's sight."

Promises of **meekness**:

Psalms 22:26
"The poor will eat and be satisfied; they who seek the LORD will praise him-- may your hearts live forever!"

Psalms 37:11
"But the meek will inherit the land and enjoy great peace."

Isaiah 11:4
"...but with righteousness he will judge the needy, with justice he will give decisions for the poor of the earth. He will strike the earth with the rod of his mouth; with the breath of his lips he will slay the wicked."

Isaiah 29:19
"Once more the humble will rejoice in the LORD; the needy will rejoice in the Holy One of Israel."

Matthew 5:5
"Blessed are the meek, for they will inherit the earth."

Examples of **meekness**:

Numbers 12:3
"(Now Moses was a very humble man, more humble than anyone else on the face of the earth.)"

2 Samuel 16:11
"David then said to Abishai and all his officials, "My son, who is of my own flesh, is trying to take my life. How much more, then, this Benjamite! Leave him alone; let him curse, for the LORD has told him to."

Acts 7:60
"Then he fell on his knees and cried out, "Lord, do not hold this sin against them." When he had said this, he fell asleep."

2 Timothy 4:16
"At my first defense, no one came to my support, but everyone deserted me. May it not be held against them."

Meekness as seen in Christ:

Isaiah 53:7
"He was oppressed and afflicted, yet he did not open his mouth; he was led like a lamb to the slaughter, and as a sheep before her shearers is silent, so he did not open his mouth."

Matthew 11:29
"Take my yoke upon you and learn from me, for I am gentle and humble in heart, and you will find rest for your souls."

Matthew 26:52
"Put your sword back in its place," Jesus said to him, "for all who draw the sword will die by the sword."

2 Corinthians 10:1
"By the meekness and gentleness of Christ, I appeal to you - I, Paul, who am 'timid' when face to face with you, but 'bold' when away!"

1 Peter 2:23
"When they hurled their insults at him, he did not retaliate; when he suffered, he made no threats. Instead, he entrusted himself to him who judges justly."

SELF-CONTROL:

Number 10 is self-control, also known as being temperate.

Self-control is literally the ability to control one's actions in such a way that what we do will be pleasing to God.

Self-control is described and discussed in:

Proverbs 16:32
"Better a patient man than a warrior, a man who controls his temper than one who takes a city."

Proverbs 21:19
"Better to live in a desert than with a quarrelsome and ill-tempered wife."

Proverbs 23:1-3

"When thou sittest to eat with a ruler, consider diligently what is before thee: And put a knife to thy throat, if thou be a man given to appetite. Be not desirous of his dainties: for they are deceitful meat."

Proverbs 25:16

"If you find honey, eat just enough - too much of it, and you will vomit."

Daniel 1:1-21

"In the third year of the reign of Jehoiakim king of Judah, Nebuchadnezzar king of Babylon came to Jerusalem and besieged it. And the Lord delivered Jehoiakim king of Judah into his hand, along with some of the articles from the temple of God. These he carried off to the temple of his god in Babylonia and put in the treasure house of his god. Then the king ordered Ashpenaz, chief of his court officials, to bring in some of the Israelites from the royal family and the nobility - young men without any physical defect, handsome, showing aptitude for every kind of learning, well informed, quick to understand, and qualified to serve in the king's palace. He was to teach them the language and literature of the Babylonians. The king assigned them a daily amount of food and wine from the king's table. They were to be trained for three years, and after that they were to enter the king's service. Among these were some from Judah: Daniel, Hananiah, Mishael and Azariah. The chief official gave them new names: to Daniel, the name Belteshazzar; to Hananiah, Shadrach; to Mishael, Meshach; and to Azariah, Abednego. But Daniel resolved not to defile himself with the royal food and wine, and he asked the chief official for permission not to defile himself this way. Now God had caused the official to show favor and sympathy to Daniel, but the official told Daniel, "I am afraid of my lord the king, who has assigned your food and drink. Why should he see you looking worse than the other young men your age? The king would then have my head because of you." Daniel then said to the guard whom the chief official had appointed over Daniel, Hananiah, Mishael and Azariah, "Please test your servants for ten days: Give us nothing but vegetables to eat and water to drink. Then compare our appearance with that of the young men who eat the royal food, and treat your servants in accordance with what you see." So he agreed to this and tested them for ten days. At the end of the ten days they looked healthier and better nourished than any of the young men who ate the royal food. So the guard took away their choice food and the wine they were to drink and gave them vegetables

instead. To these four young men God gave knowledge and understanding of all kinds of literature and learning. And Daniel could understand visions and dreams of all kinds. At the end of the time set by the king to bring them in, the chief official presented them to Nebuchadnezzar. The king talked with them, and he found none equal to Daniel, Hananiah, Mishael and Azariah; so they entered the king's service. In every matter of wisdom and understanding about which the king questioned them, he found them ten times better than all the magicians and enchanters in his whole kingdom. And Daniel remained there until the first year of King Cyrus."

Acts 24:25
"As Paul discoursed on righteousness, self-control and the judgment to come, Felix was afraid and said, "That's enough for now! You may leave. When I find it convenient, I will send for you."

James 2:2
"For in many things we offend all. If any man offend not in word, the same is a perfect man, and able also to bridle the whole body."

Titus 2:2
"Teach the older men to be temperate, worthy of respect, self-controlled, and sound in faith, in love and in endurance."

2 Peter 1:5-7
"For this very reason, make every effort to add to your faith goodness; and to goodness, knowledge; and to knowledge, self-control; and to self-control, perseverance; and to perseverance, godliness; and to godliness, brotherly kindness; and to brotherly kindness, love."

Self-control is a must for every child of God. We learn it best by going through the wilderness experience.

MERCY:

Mercy is described as leniency shown to a guilty person or living compassionately towards others. Let me describe the difference between Grace and Mercy. Grace is getting what you don't deserve. Mercy is not getting what you deserve.

159

The Scriptures speak of mercy in:

1 Samuel 11:13
"But Saul said, "No one shall be put to death today, for this day the LORD has rescued Israel."

1 Samuel 26:9
"But David said to Abishai, "Don't destroy him! Who can lay a hand on the Lord's anointed and be guiltless?"

2 Samuel 19:22
"David replied, "What do you and I have in common, you sons of Zeruiah? This day you have become my adversaries! Should anyone be put to death in Israel today? Do I not know that today I am king over Israel?"

1 Kings 1:52
"Solomon replied, "If he shows himself to be a worthy man, not a hair of his head will fall to the ground; but if evil is found in him, he will die."

2 Kings 6:22
"Do not kill them," he answered. "Would you kill men you have captured with your own sword or bow? Set food and water before them so that they may eat and drink and then go back to their master."

John 8:7
"When they kept on questioning him, he straightened up and said to them, "If any one of you is without sin, let him be the first to throw a stone at her."

The lack of **mercy**:

Deuteronomy 4:31
"For the LORD your God is a merciful God; he will not abandon or destroy you or forget the covenant with your forefathers, which he confirmed to them by oath."

2 Samuel 24:14
"David said to Gad, "I am in deep distress. Let us fall into the hands of the LORD, for his mercy is great; but do not let me fall into the hands of

men."

Psalms 86:5
"You are forgiving and good, O Lord, abounding in love to all who call to you."

Psalms 103:17
"But from everlasting to everlasting the Lord's love is with those who fear him, and his righteousness with their children's children..."

Psalms 108:4
"For great is your love, higher than the heavens; your faithfulness reaches to the skies."

Lamentations 3:22-23
"Because of the Lord's great love we are not consumed, for his compassions never fail. They are new every morning; great is your faithfulness."

Job 2:13
"Then they sat on the ground with him for seven days and seven nights. No one said a word to him, because they saw how great his suffering was."

Micah 7:18
"Who is a God like you, who pardons sin and forgives the transgression of the remnant of his inheritance? You do not stay angry forever but delight to show mercy."

Titus 3:5
"...he saved us, not because of righteous things we had done, but because of his mercy. He saved us through the washing of rebirth and renewal by the Holy Spirit."

More **mercy**:

Proverbs 3:3
"Let love and faithfulness never leave you; bind them around your neck, write them on the tablet of your heart."

Proverbs 11:17
"A kind man benefits himself, but a cruel man brings trouble on himself."

Micah 6:8
"He has showed you, O man, what is good. And what does the LORD require of you? To act justly and to love mercy and to walk humbly with your God."

Matthew 5:7
"Blessed are the merciful, for they will be shown mercy."

Luke 6:36
"Be merciful, just as your Father is merciful."

Mercy defined:

Exodus 34:7
"...maintaining love to thousands, and forgiving wickedness, rebellion and sin. Yet he does not leave the guilty unpunished; he punishes the children and their children for the sin of the fathers to the third and fourth generation."

2 Samuel 22:26
"To the faithful you show yourself faithful, to the blameless you show yourself blameless."

2 Chronicles 30:9
"If you return to the LORD, then your brothers and your children will be shown compassion by their captors and will come back to this land, for the LORD your God is gracious and compassionate. He will not turn his face from you if you return to him."

Psalms 89:28
"I will maintain my love to him forever, and my covenant with him will never fail."

Psalms 103:8
"The LORD is compassionate and gracious, slow to anger, abounding in love."

Isaiah 54:7
"For a brief moment I abandoned you, but with deep compassion I will bring you back."

Isaiah 55:7
"Let the wicked forsake his way and the evil man his thoughts. Let him turn to the LORD, and he will have mercy on him, and to our God, for he will freely pardon."

Jeremiah 3:12
"Go, proclaim this message toward the north :"Return, faithless Israel," declares the LORD, "I will frown on you no longer, for I am merciful," declares the LORD, "I will not be angry forever."

We need to be merciful. Jesus said that for those who are merciful, they shall obtain mercy. We all need mercy especially when we're in a position where we could easily be judged and condemned because of our actions or attitudes. We thank God for His mercy.

WISDOM:

Wisdom is applied knowledge in given situations. The Holy Spirit is described in the Old Testament as wisdom. You need the wisdom of the Holy Spirit to function properly.

Wisdom is discussed in:

Psalms 104:24
"How many are your works, O LORD! In wisdom you made them all; the earth is full of your creatures."

Proverbs 3:19
"By wisdom the LORD laid the earth's foundations, by understanding he set the heavens in place."

Proverbs 4:7
"Wisdom is supreme; therefore get wisdom. Though it cost all you have, get understanding."

Job 28:28
"And he said to man "The fear of the Lord - that is wisdom, and to shun evil is understanding."

Job 32:7
"I thought, "Age should speak; advanced years should teach wisdom."

Isaiah 11:2
"The Spirit of the LORD will rest on him - the Spirit of wisdom and of understanding, the Spirit of counsel and of power, the Spirit of knowledge and of the fear of the LORD..."

Hosea 14:9
"Who is wise? He will realize these things. Who is discerning? He will understand them. The ways of the LORD are right; the righteous walk in them, but the rebellious stumble in them."

Matthew 7:24
"Therefore everyone who hears these words of mine and puts them into practice is like a wise man who built his house on the rock."

Matthew 13:54
"Coming to his hometown, he began teaching the people in their synagogue, and they were amazed. "Where did this man get this wisdom and these miraculous powers?" they asked."

Luke 2:40
"And the child grew and became strong; he was filled with wisdom, and the grace of God was upon him."

1 Corinthians 1:24
"...but to those whom God has called, both Jews and Greeks, Christ the power of God and the wisdom of God."

1 Corinthians 1:25
"For the foolishness of God is wiser than man's wisdom, and the weakness of God is stronger than man's strength."

Romans 11:33
"Oh, the depth of the riches of the wisdom and knowledge of God! How un-searchable his judgments, and his paths beyond tracing out!"

Colossians 2:3
"...in whom are hidden all the treasures of wisdom and knowledge."

James 3:17
"But the wisdom that comes from heaven is first of all pure; then peace-loving, considerate, submissive, full of mercy and good fruit, impartial and sincere."

2 Timothy 3:15
"...and how from infancy you have known the holy Scriptures, which are able to make you wise for salvation through faith in Christ Jesus."

The Bible says pray for **wisdom:**

2 Chronicles 1:10
"Give me wisdom and knowledge, that I may lead this people, for who is able to govern this great people of yours?"

Psalms 90:12
"Teach us to number our days aright, that we may gain a heart of wisdom."

Proverbs 2:3
"If you accept my words and store up my commands within you, turning your ear to wisdom and applying your heart to understanding."

Ephesians 1:17
"I keep asking that the God of our Lord Jesus Christ, the glorious Father, may give you the Spirit of wisdom and revelation, so that you may know him better."

Colossians 1:9
"For this reason, since the day we heard about you, we have not stopped praying for you and asking God to fill you with the knowledge of his will through all spiritual wisdom and understanding."

James 1:5
"If any of you lacks wisdom, he should ask God, who gives generously to all without finding fault, and it will be given to him."

The preciousness of **wisdom**:

Proverbs 3:13-14
"Blessed is the man who finds wisdom, the man who gains understanding, for she is more profitable than silver and yields better returns than gold."

Proverbs 8:11
"...for wisdom is more precious than rubies, and nothing you desire can compare with her."

Ecclesiastes 2:13
"I saw that wisdom is better than folly, just as light is better than darkness."

Ecclesiastes 7:19
"Wisdom makes one wise man more powerful than ten rulers in a city."

Wisdom is promised to us:

Proverbs 2:6
"For the LORD gives wisdom, and from his mouth come knowledge and understanding."

Proverbs 2:7
"He holds victory in store for the upright, he is a shield to those whose walk is blameless."

Ecclesiastes 2:26
"To the man who pleases him, God gives wisdom, knowledge and happiness, but to the sinner he gives the task of gathering and storing up wealth to hand it over to the one who pleases God. This too is meaningless, a chasing after the wind."

Daniel 2:21
"He changes times and seasons; he sets up kings and deposes them. He

gives wisdom to the wise and knowledge to the discerning."

Luke 21:15
"For I will give you words and wisdom that none of your adversaries will be able to resist or contradict."

Examples of **wisdom**:

1 Kings 4:30
"Solomon's wisdom was greater than the wisdom of all the men of the East, and greater than all the wisdom of Egypt."

1 Kings 10:3
"Solomon answered all her questions; nothing was too hard for the king to explain to her."

Daniel 1:20
"In every matter of wisdom and understanding about which the king questioned them, he found them ten times better than all the magicians and enchanters in his whole kingdom."

Acts 6:10
"...but they could not stand up against his wisdom or the Spirit by whom he spoke."

KNOWLEDGE:

The 13th characteristic of the heart that we are to apply to 40 Days to the Promise process is knowledge. Knowledge is more than the intellectual gathering of facts. It means to know by experience.

In and of itself, **knowledge,** can be a hindrance:

Genesis 3:5-6 & 22-23
"For God knows that when you eat of it your eyes will be opened, and you will be like God, knowing good and evil. When the woman saw that the fruit of the tree was good for food and pleasing to the eye, and also desirable for gaining wisdom, she took some and ate it. She also gave some to her husband, who was with her, and he ate it. And the LORD God

said, "The man has now become like one of us, knowing good and evil. He must not be allowed to reach out his hand and take also from the tree of life and eat, and live forever. So the LORD God banished him from the Garden of Eden to work the ground from which he had been taken."

Ecclesiastes 1:18
"For with much wisdom comes much sorrow; the more knowledge, the more grief."

Ecclesiastes 12:12
"Be warned, my son, of anything in addition to them. Of making many books there is no end, and much study wearies the body."

1 Corinthians 8:1
"Now about food sacrificed to idols: We know that we all possess knowledge. Knowledge puffs up, but love builds up."

Mere **human knowledge** can be vague and worthless:

Isaiah 44:25
"…who foils the signs of false prophets and makes fools of diviners, who overthrows the learning of the wise and turns it into nonsense,"

1 Corinthians 8:2
"The man who thinks he knows something does not yet know as he ought to know."

1 Corinthians 13:8
"Love never fails. But where there are prophecies, they will cease; where there are tongues, they will be stilled; where there is knowledge, it will pass away."

The pursuit of **knowledge** is joy:

Proverbs 2:3
"…and if you call out for insight and cry aloud for understanding,"

Proverbs 3:13
"Blessed is the man who finds wisdom, the man who gains

understanding,"

Proverbs 4:5
"Get wisdom, get understanding; do not forget my words or swerve from them."

Proverbs 15:14 (knowledge)
"The discerning heart seeks knowledge, but the mouth of a fool feeds on folly."

Proverbs 23:23 (wisdom)
"Buy the truth and do not sell it; get wisdom, discipline and understanding."

2 Peter 1:5 (gifts of faith)
"For this very reason, make every effort to add to your faith goodness; and to goodness, knowledge;"

Seek **spiritual knowledge**:

Jeremiah 9:24
"...but let him who boasts boast about this: that he understands and knows me, that I am the LORD, who exercises kindness, justice and righteousness on earth, for in these I delight," declares the LORD.

Hosea 6:3
"Let us acknowledge the LORD; let us press on to acknowledge him. As surely as the sun rises, he will appear; he will come to us like the winter rains, like the spring rains that water the earth."

References to **intellectual knowledge**:

Proverbs 1:4
"...for giving prudence to the simple, knowledge and discretion to the young..."

Proverbs 2:10
"For wisdom will enter your heart, and knowledge will be pleasant to your soul."

Proverbs 14:6
"The mocker seeks wisdom and finds none, but knowledge comes easily to the discerning."

Proverbs 15:7
"The lips of the wise spread knowledge; not so the hearts of fools."

Proverbs 24:4
"...through knowledge its rooms are filled with rare and beautiful treasures."

Daniel 1:4-5
"...young men without any physical defect, handsome, showing aptitude for every kind of learning, well informed, quick to understand, and qualified to serve in the king's palace. He was to teach them the language and literature of the Babylonians. The king assigned them a daily amount of food and wine from the king's table. They were to be trained for three years, and after that they were to enter the king's service."

Daniel 12:4
"But you, Daniel, close up and seal the words of the scroll until the time of the end. Many will go here and there to increase knowledge."

Knowledge from God:

Daniel 1:17
"To these four young men God gave knowledge and understanding of all kinds of literature and learning. And Daniel could understand visions and dreams of all kinds."

TRUTH:

Throughout the process of the 40 days to the promise, is the search for truth. Truth about the issues of your heart.

Jesus said that He is the way, the truth and the life. It is through truth that we come to a place of knowing and embracing the life of God.

170

The following scriptures speak of **Truth**:

Psalms 119:72
"The law from your mouth is more precious to me than thousands of pieces of silver and gold."

Psalms 119:127
"Because I love your commands more than gold, more than pure gold,"

Psalms 119:162
"I rejoice in your promise like one who finds great spoil."

Proverbs 23:23
"Buy the truth and do not sell it; get wisdom, discipline and understanding."

The attitude of the wicked shows how significant truth is!

The importance of **truth:**

Isaiah 59:4
"No one calls for justice; no one pleads his case with integrity. They rely on empty arguments and speak lies; they conceive trouble and give birth to evil."

Jeremiah 9:5
"Friend deceives friend, and no one speaks the truth. They have taught their tongues to lie; they weary themselves with sinning."

Galatians 3:1-5
"You foolish Galatians! Who has bewitched you? Before your very eyes Jesus Christ was clearly portrayed as crucified. I would like to learn just one thing from you: Did you receive the Spirit by observing the law, or by believing what you heard? Are you so foolish? After beginning with the Spirit, are you now trying to attain your goal by human effort? Have you suffered so much for nothing--if it really was for nothing? Does God give you his Spirit and work miracles among you because you observe the law, or because you believe what you heard?"

2 Thessalonians 2:9-10
"The coming of the lawless one will be in accordance with the work of Satan displayed in all kinds of counterfeit miracles, signs and wonders, and in every sort of evil that deceives those who are perishing. They perish because they refused to love the truth and so be saved."

1 Timothy 6:3-5
"If anyone teaches false doctrines and does not agree to the sound instruction of our Lord Jesus Christ and to godly teaching, he is conceited and understands nothing. He has an unhealthy interest in controversies and quarrels about words that result in envy, strife, malicious talk, evil suspicions and constant friction between men of corrupt mind, who have been robbed of the truth and who think that godliness is a means to financial gain."

2 Timothy 3:8
"Just as Jannes and Jambres opposed Moses, so also these men oppose the truth--men of depraved minds, who, as far as the faith is concerned, are rejected."

HOPE:

The Bible says that hope deferred makes the heart sick (Prov. 13:12). When you hope for something to come to pass and it doesn't, you can become discouraged and disheartened.

Many people have lost all hope. One of the characteristics of a Christian's heart is to be filled with hope knowing that God will fulfill His promises.

Hope is discussed in:

Romans 8:24
"For in this hope we were saved. But hope that is seen is no hope at all. Who hopes for what he already has?"

Romans 15:4
"For everything that was written in the past was written to teach us, so that through endurance and the encouragement of the Scriptures we

might have hope."

1 Corinthians 13:13
"And now these three remain: faith, hope and love. But the greatest of these is love."

Acts 24:15
"...and I have the same hope in God as these men, that there will be a resurrection of both the righteous and the wicked."

Colossians 1:3-5
"We always thank God, the Father of our Lord Jesus Christ, when we pray for you, because we have heard of your faith in Christ Jesus and of the love you have for all the saints - the faith and love that spring from the hope that is stored up for you in heaven and that you have already heard about in the word of truth, the gospel."

Titus 2:13
"...while we wait for the blessed hope - the glorious appearing of our great God and Savior, Jesus Christ...,"

Hebrews 6:18-19
"God did this so that, by two unchangeable things in which it is impossible for God to lie, we who have fled to take hold of the hope offered to us may be greatly encouraged. We have this hope as an anchor for the soul, firm and secure. It enters the inner sanctuary behind the curtain,..."

1 Peter 1:3
"Praise be to the God and Father of our Lord Jesus Christ! In his great mercy he has given us new birth into a living hope through the resurrection of Jesus Christ from the dead,"

1 Peter 3:15
"But in your hearts set apart Christ as Lord. Always be prepared to give an answer to everyone who asks you to give the reason for the hope that you have. But do this with gentleness and respect..."

1 John 3:3
"Everyone who has this hope in him purifies himself, just as he is pure."

Our **hope** is in God:

Jeremiah 17:7
"But blessed is the man who trusts in the LORD, whose confidence is in him."

Psalms 31:24
"Be strong and take heart, all you who hope in the LORD."

Psalms 33:18
"But the eyes of the LORD are on those who fear him, on those whose hope is in his unfailing love…,"

Psalms 39:7
"But now, Lord, what do I look for? My hope is in you."

Psalms 41:11
"I know that you are pleased with me, for my enemy does not triumph over me."

Psalms 71:5
"For you have been my hope, O Sovereign LORD, my confidence since my youth."

Psalms 146:5
"Blessed is he whose help is the God of Jacob, whose hope is in the LORD his God,"

As the writer of the beautiful old hymn penned, "My **hope** is built on nothing less than Jesus' blood and righteousness; I dare not trust the sweetest frame, but wholly lean on Jesus, name." Your hope must be anchored in Jesus Christ!

CONTENTMENT:

The Bible says, "godliness with contentment is great gain" I Tim. 6:6.

To rest and be satisfied in what God has given to you is a Christian goal. You can be so filled with ambition, desire to succeed and move ahead in your life that you miss the relationship with God you are truly desiring.

Ambition is a positive trait in business and industry, but God wants to bring you to a place of contentment in Him. It is akin to peace but it really means laying aside your own ambition to hear from the Lord and to live according to His perfect plan.

Scripturally we see contentment in:

Proverbs 15:16
"Better a little with the fear of the LORD than great wealth with turmoil."

Luke 3:14
"Then some soldiers asked him, "And what should we do?" He replied, "Don't extort money and don't accuse people falsely - be content with your pay."

Philippians 4:11
"I am not saying this because I am in need, for I have learned to be content whatever the circumstances."

1 Timothy 6:6
"But godliness with contentment is great gain."

1 Timothy 6:8
"But if we have food and clothing, we will be content with that."

Hebrews 13:5
"Keep your lives free from the love of money and be content with what you have, because God has said, "Never will I leave you; never will I forsake you."

His **rest**:

Exodus 33:14
The LORD replied, "My Presence will go with you, and I will give you rest."

175

Psalms 116:7
"*Be at rest once more, O my soul, for the LORD has been good to you.*"

Isaiah 28:12
"*...to whom he said, "This is the resting place, let the weary rest," and, "This is the place of repose" - but they would not listen.*"

Matthew 11:29
"*Take my yoke upon you and learn from me, for I am gentle and humble in heart, and you will find rest for your souls.*"

Hebrews 4:3
"*Now we who have believed enter that rest, just as God has said, "So I declared on oath in my anger, 'They shall never enter my rest.' " And yet his work has been finished since the creation of the world.*"

Revelation 14:13
"*Then I heard a voice from heaven say, "Write: Blessed are the dead who die in the Lord from now on." "Yes," says the Spirit, "they will rest from their labor, for their deeds will follow them.*"

Satisfaction:

Psalms 36:8
"*They feast on the abundance of your house; you give them drink from your river of delights.*"

Psalms 63:5
"*My soul will be satisfied as with the richest of foods; with singing lips my mouth will praise you.*"

Psalms 103:5
"*...who satisfies your desires with good things so that your youth is renewed like the eagles.*"

Psalms 107:9
"*...for he satisfies the thirsty and fills the hungry with good things.*"

Isaiah 58:11
"The LORD will guide you always; he will satisfy your needs in a sun-scorched land and will strengthen your frame. You will be like a well-watered garden, like a spring whose waters never fail."

Isaiah 55:1
"Come, all you who are thirsty, come to the waters; and you who have no money, come, buy and eat! Come, buy wine and milk without money and without cost."

Matthew 5:6
"Blessed are those who hunger and thirst for righteousness, for they will be filled."

John 4:14
"...but whoever drinks the water I give him will never thirst. Indeed, the water I give him will become in him a spring of water welling up to eternal life."

John 7:37
On the last and greatest day of the Feast, Jesus stood and said in a loud voice, "If anyone is thirsty, let him come to me and drink."

Revelation 7:16
"Never again will they hunger; never again will they thirst. The sun will not beat upon them, nor any scorching heat."

Revelation 22:17
"The Spirit and the bride say, "Come!" And let him who hears say, "Come!" Whoever is thirsty, let him come; and whoever wishes, let him take the free gift of the water of life."

HUMILITY:

Number 17 is humility. Humility is defined as a person who is humble, lowly or meek. A person who is modest. Certainly not proud, arrogant, or assuming. People who are constantly seeking attention are usually the opposite of humble. Humility is a tremendous characteristic of a Christian's life.

We see **humility** in:

Proverbs 16:19
"Better to be lowly in spirit and among the oppressed than to share plunder with the proud."

Proverbs 22:4
"Humility and the fear of the LORD bring wealth and honor and life."

Proverbs 29:23
"A man's pride brings him low, but a man of lowly spirit gains honor."

Isaiah 57:15
"For this is what the high and lofty One says - he who lives forever, whose name is holy: "I live in a high and holy place, but also with him who is contrite and lowly in spirit, to revive the spirit of the lowly and to revive the heart of the contrite."

Micah 6:8
"He has showed you, O man, what is good. And what does the LORD require of you? To act justly and to love mercy and to walk humbly with your God."

Matthew 18:4
"Therefore, whoever humbles himself like this child is the greatest in the kingdom of heaven."

Luke 14:10
"But when you are invited, take the lowest place, so that when your host comes, he will say to you, "Friend, move up to a better place." Then you will be honored in the presence of all your fellow guests."

Luke 22:26
"But you are not to be like that. Instead, the greatest among you should be like the youngest, and the one who rules like the one who serves."

Romans 12:3
"For by the grace given me I say to every one of you: Do not think of yourself more highly than you ought, but rather think of yourself with

sober judgment, in accordance with the measure of faith God has given you."

James 4:10
"Humble yourselves before the Lord, and he will lift you up."

1 Peter 5:5
"Young men, in the same way be submissive to those who are older. All of you, clothe yourselves with humility toward one another, because, "God opposes the proud but gives grace to the humble."

FORGIVENESS:

Forgiveness is the fruit of true confession and repentance. You must learn to forgive those who have offended you for as you forgive so shall you be forgiven.

Forgiveness is seen in:

Psalms 34:18
"The LORD is close to the brokenhearted and saves those who are crushed in spirit."

Psalms 51:7
"Cleanse me with hyssop, and I will be clean; wash me, and I will be whiter than snow."

Psalms 103:3
"...who forgives all your sins and heals all your diseases,"

Psalms 130:4
"But with you there is forgiveness; therefore you are feared."

Matthew 6:14
"For if you forgive men when they sin against you, your heavenly Father will also forgive you."

Mark 11:25
"And when you stand praying, if you hold anything against anyone,

forgive him, so that your Father in heaven may forgive you your sins."

Luke 17:4
"If he sins against you seven times in a day, and seven times comes back to you and says, 'I repent,' forgive him."

Acts 3:19
"Repent, then, and turn to God, so that your sins may be wiped out, that times of refreshing may come from the Lord."

Acts 5:31
"God exalted him to his own right hand as Prince and Savior that he might give repentance and forgiveness of sins to Israel."

Acts 13:38
"Therefore, my brothers, I want you to know that through Jesus the forgiveness of sins is proclaimed to you."

Ephesians 1:7
"In him we have redemption through his blood, the forgiveness of sins, in accordance with the riches of God's grace."

Colossians 3:13
"Bear with each other and forgive whatever grievances you may have against one another. Forgive as the Lord forgave you."

1 John 1:9
"If we confess our sins, he is faithful and just and will forgive us our sins and purify us from all unrighteousness."

The more quickly you forgive others you also will be forgiven. Forgiveness should be a part of your Christian lifestyle.

So in terms of this day's journey, you need to think of the people who have offended you or perhaps that you have offended. As you do, pray a prayer of forgiveness. Release each person before the Lord.

RIGHTEOUSNESS:

Righteousness is living right or being in right standing with God. Your righteousness has been given to you through the blood of Jesus and your relationship with Him. You did not earn righteousness, it is provided freely.

You are saved not by the works of your righteousness but by God's grace and tender mercy.

Righteousness in the Bible is seen in:

Psalms 48:10
"Like your name, O God, your praise reaches to the ends of the earth; your right hand is filled with righteousness."

Psalms 97:2
"Clouds and thick darkness surround him; righteousness and justice are the foundation of his throne."

Psalms 119:137
"Righteous are you, O LORD, and your laws are right."

Psalms 45:7
"You love righteousness and hate wickedness; therefore God, your God, has set you above your companions by anointing you with the oil of joy."

Isaiah 59:16
"He saw that there was no one, he was appalled that there was no one to intervene; so his own arm worked salvation for him, and his own righteousness sustained him."

Jeremiah 23:5-6
"The days are coming," declares the LORD, "when I will raise up to David a righteous Branch, a King who will reign wisely and do what is just and right in the land. In his days Judah will be saved and Israel will live in safety. This is the name by which he will be called: The LORD Our Righteousness."

Hosea 10:12
"Sow for yourselves righteousness, reap the fruit of unfailing love, and break up your unplowed ground; for it is time to seek the LORD, until he comes and showers righteousness on you."

Matthew 5:20
"For I tell you that unless your righteousness surpasses that of the Pharisees and the teachers of the law, you will certainly not enter the kingdom of heaven."

Ephesians 6:13-14 (KJV)
"Wherefore take unto you the whole armor of God, that ye may be able to withstand in the evil day, and having done all, to stand. Stand therefore, having your loins gird about with truth, and having on the breastplate of righteousness..."

Philippians 1:11
"...filled with the fruit of righteousness that comes through Jesus Christ - to the glory and praise of God."

God wants you to walk in righteousness!

Notice what Paul the Apostle said: "...put on the new man, which after God is created in righteousness and true holiness" Ephesians 4:24 KJV.

You are striving to have right thinking. Following right thinking will come right behavior.

JUSTICE:

Justice is defined as the quality of being just or showing equity, merited, reward or punishment, the administration of the law, or a judge, a magistrate. Justice means to do something that is equal.

In the world there is a tremendous lack of justice. Justice and equality in terms of social systems, in terms of racial equality, etc.

One of the indictments against the church today is the lack of justice, or the mistreatment of women, children and those of racial or cultural diversity. This is a sin in that we need to repent of because it keeps us from fulfilling God's plan as a nation and His glorious church.

The Scriptures speak of **divine justice** in:

Psalms 103:6
"The LORD works righteousness and justice for all the oppressed."

Zephaniah 3:5
"The LORD within her is righteous; he does no wrong. Morning by morning he dispenses his justice, and every new day he does not fail, yet the unrighteous know no shame."

John 5:30
"By myself I can do nothing; I judge only as I hear, and my judgment is just, for I seek not to please myself but him who sent me."

Romans 2:2
"Now we know that God's judgment against those who do such things is based on truth."

Justice is urged:

Deuteronomy 16:20
"Follow justice and justice alone, so that you may live and possess the land the LORD your God is giving you."

Psalms 82:3
"Defend the cause of the weak and fatherless; maintain the rights of the poor and oppressed."

Proverbs 21:3
"To do what is right and just is more acceptable to the LORD than sacrifice."

Isaiah 56:1
This is what the LORD says: "Maintain justice and do what is right, for my salvation is close at hand and my righteousness will soon be revealed."

Romans 13:7
"Give everyone what you owe him: If you owe taxes, pay taxes; if revenue, then revenue; if respect, then respect; if honor, then honor."

Colossians 4:1
"Masters, provide your slaves with what is right and fair, because you know that you also have a Master in heaven."

Human justice:

2 Samuel 8:15
"David reigned over all Israel, doing what was just and right for all his people."

1 Kings 1:52
Solomon replied, "If he shows himself to be a worthy man, not a hair of his head will fall to the ground; but if evil is found in him, he will die."

1 Kings 3:28
"When all Israel heard the verdict the king had given, they held the king in awe, because they saw that he had wisdom from God to administer justice."

2 Kings 14:6
"Yet he did not put the sons of the assassins to death, in accordance with what is written in the Book of the Law of Moses where the LORD commanded: "Fathers shall not be put to death for their children, nor children put to death for their fathers; each is to die for his own sins."

Jeremiah 22:15
"Does it make you a king to have more and more cedar? Did not your father have food and drink? He did what was right and just, so all went well with him."

Acts 25:16

"I told them that it is not the Roman custom to hand over any man before he has faced his accusers and has had an opportunity to defend himself against their charges."

CONCLUSION:

As I mentioned before, the process that you are going to go through is put off the old, renew your mind, and put on the new. You are giving careful study to 2 cycles of 20, one of each on a daily basis for at least a 1/2 hour.

Read the Scriptures and pray regarding a negative characteristic that needs to be put off then a positive characteristic that needs to be put on and apply it to your heart.

In the next chapter we will look at how the 40 day plan works and what the expected results should be.

CHAPTER TWELVE

The 40 Day Plan

Based upon James 5, and 1 John 1:9, it is important that you find a caring individual who is mature in the Lord with whom you can go through this process. Even a small group of 2 or 3 can work through these steps in a fairly consistent pattern.

Take one section at a time.

Example: Day number one begin with immorality and love.

First, you are going to put off immorality. You may be asking, how do we put off immorality? The putting off process means to confess or to speak it out.

You either confess or admit that immorality is an issue or that it ever was an issue in your heart. You then come into a prayer of agreement with your partner, stating, "I put off immorality in the name of Jesus Christ."

Keep in mind that this is not an accusation against you that you are or ever have been immoral. If this sin has never been a part of your life, in thought or deed, then thank God for keeping you clean and continue with your journey.

After reading the Scriptures pray that God will break any generational curse that may be upon your life from past sins. Allow the Holy Spirit to cleanse you by God's word and by the blood of Jesus Christ.

Next you put on love. Putting on is two fold. First you speak it, "Lord, you called me to love you with all of my heart and to love my neighbor as myself. I put on love and I am accepted in the name of Jesus."

Second, pray that God will help you to act in love in your daily walk. You must do more than just say it. God wants you to do it. The "working out process" takes time.

You proceed one day at a time dealing with the Scriptures first then pray and come into agreement with your partner or counselor that God will help you to be conformed to the image of Christ.

All the things that you put off are part of your old carnal nature. While the things you put on are the new man, the spiritual man. In putting off the old you actually get rid of the negative aspects of your character that have been sown in your life through past experiences.

Through confessing the truth of God's Word in terms of your new character in Christ, you are sowing new seeds: seeds of promise and hope that will bring forth fruit which will remain. It is God's plan and purpose not to just change your behavior, but first to change your heart which will lead you into a change in the way you act and respond.

The 40 day plan requires the participant to purchase the *40 Days to the Promise Journal* available from Vision Publishing.

In the study guide each of the 40 characteristics of the heart, the negative and the positive are listed out for you with places to write so that you can record what God is saying to you as you go through the process.

On the pages of the study guide you can admit your failures, confess the sin and receive cleansing from God. At the same time, you are going to not only speak out and put off the old nature and put on the new self but you are to write down the things that you can do to exhibit that characteristic in your daily life.

As you do this you will be actively participating with the work of the Holy Spirit to bring about change and transformation in your character. This will help you move through your wilderness so that you do not have to take a 40 year trek in the wilderness instead you will take a 40 day trip to prepare yourself to inherit the promises of God.

CHAPTER THIRTEEN

Expected Results

Each individual is different. Some of the people who have gone through this process have seen dramatic results in their lives and likewise in the lives of others. Much depends on the level of disturbance or difficulty that you have carried from your old carnal nature.

If your life has been fairly free of sin and sinful behavior there's less likelihood that this will make a major difference in you. But for those who have had significant troubles it can bring dramatic change.

One thing is certain, going through this process will help you to know beyond a shadow of a doubt that you have dealt with the issues of your heart.

Through prayer and the study of God's Word you will learn what He expects and you will have the tools to live according to His plan. Whenever the devil tries to condemn you for past wrongs, you can remind him of your Journey to freedom.

You will live according to Paul the Apostle's declaration:

> *"There is therefore now no condemnation to them which are in Christ Jesus, who walk not after the flesh but after the Spirit."* Romans 8:1 KJV

It is my hope that you will receive great results. Results that will be positive for your future development because it is God's plan that you inherit the promises. God's promises include eternal life, which begins the moment you accept Christ as your Savior.

His promises include abundance, prosperity, the ability to rule and reign with Christ and the establishment of God's kingdom here on earth. God has given us many tools to be able to function inside

Canaan.

As you move in and start inheriting the Promised Land you will need to put on the whole armor of God because that's when the real battles begin. God does not want you to face the battles alone. He wants you to be prepared, transformed, hardened, and strong in the Lord and in the power of His might so you will be victorious in what He calls you to do.

It is important to remember that it took a long time to develop the character you have and it's going to take time for the transformation process to work. So, trust the procedure. God is doing a great work in you and as you are obedient to walk in His ways He will complete His mighty work.

It is important to realize that God loves you. His love for you will never change. No matter what you do, no matter how often you might falter and fail, He still loves you! His love is everlasting. He loves you more then you can ever imagine. He has proven His great love by adopting you as His own. He chose you, cleansed you and made you acceptable in the Beloved.

God has given you a great inheritance! He wants you, as part of His glorious church, to enjoy your inheritance to its fullest. You are an important member of His eternal Kingdom. By the blood of Jesus you are a child of the King so live like a prince or a princess!

An old Chinese proverb says: "A thousand mile journey begins with one step!" Are you ready to begin your journey of a lifetime? If you are…take the first step and don't quit until you hear the Master say *"Well done my good and faithful servant!"*

193

Printed in the United States
24821LVS00003B/34-57